Get started in French

Catrine Carpenter

Advisory editor
Paul Coggle

Revised by
Bruno Paul

For UK order enquiries: please contact Bookpoint Ltd, 130 Milton Park, Abingdon, Oxon OX14 4SB. *Telephone:* +44 (0) 1235 827720. *Fax:* +44 (0) 1235 400454. Lines are open 09.00–17.00, Monday to Saturday, with a 24-hour message answering service. Details about our titles and how to order are available at www.teachyourself.co.uk

For USA order enquiries: please contact McGraw-Hill Customer Services, PO Box 545, Blacklick, OH 43004-0545, USA. *Telephone:* 1-800-722-4726. *Fax:* 1-614-755-5645.

For Canada order enquiries: please contact McGraw-Hill Ryerson Ltd, 300 Water St, Whitby, Ontario L1N 9B6, Canada. *Telephone:* 905 430 5000. *Fax:* 905 430 5020.

Long renowned as the authoritative source for self-guided learning – with more than 50 million copies sold worldwide – the *teach yourself* series includes over 500 titles in the fields of languages, crafts, hobbies, business, computing and education.

British Library Cataloguing in Publication Data: a catalogue record for this title is available from the British Library.

Library of Congress Catalog Card Number: on file.

First published in UK 1992 by Hodder Education, part of Hachette Livre UK, 338 Euston Road, London, NW1 3BH.

First published in US 1992 by The McGraw-Hill Companies, Inc.

This edition published 2012.

Previously published as Teach Yourself Beginner's French

The *Teach Yourself* name is a registered trade mark of Hodder Headline.

Typeset by Integra Software Services Pvt. Ltd., Pondicherry, India.

Illustrated by Barking Dog Art, Sally Elford, Peter Lubach.

Printed in China for Hodder Education, an Hachette Livre UK Company, 338 Euston Road, London NW1 3BH.

The publisher has used its best endeavours to ensure that the URLs for external websites referred to in this book are correct and active at the time of going to press. However, the publisher and the author have no responsibility for the websites and can make no guarantee that a site will remain live or that the content will remain relevant, decent or appropriate.

Hachette Livre UK's policy is to use papers that are natural, renewable and recyclable products and made from wood grown in sustainable forests. The logging and manufacturing processes are expected to conform to the environmental regulations of the country of origin.

Impression number   10 9 8 7 6 5 4

Year 2014

Contents

Meet the author   **vi**

How to use this book   **vii**

Learn to learn   **x**

Pronunciation guide   **xiv**

Useful expressions   **xvii**

1 **Bonjour** *Hello*
Simple questions • Refusing politely in French • How
to be courteous • When to use **tu**; when to use **vous**   **2**

2 **C'est combien?** *How much is it?*
A, an • *The*: **le, la, l', les** • *Some, any* • *One/a/an*
• *How much is it?* • Numbers up to ten   **10**

3 **Je m'appelle ... et vous?** *My name is ... what's yours?*
Regular verbs ending in **-er** • Two important verbs:
to have, to be • The negative form • Numbers 11–20
• Adjectives: their agreement • Capital letters
• Saying how old you are   **18**

Review 1   **28**

4 **Vous habitez où?** *Where do you live?*
How to ask simple questions • *Is it ...? Is that ...?*
• *Is there ...? Are there ...?* • Other questions
• *My, your, his* • Numbers 20–70   **30**

5 **Quelle heure est-il?** *What time is it?*
Days of the week • Months of the year • Numbers
70–90 • Saying what you want/want to do • Three
different ways to ask a question • Questions starting
with *what* • Verbs ending in **-ir** and **-re** • Giving the
date • Telling the time ·*To do/to make* • *To take*   **40**

6 **Pour aller à ...?** *The way to ...?*
Asking the way and giving directions • *To go, to leave*
• Understanding directions • When to use **à**; when
to use **en** • When **à** is followed by **le, la, l', les**
• Locating the exact spot • Numbers 90 upwards
• *First, second, third* **52**

7 **C'est comment?** *What is it like?*
Colours •*This, that, these, those* • Saying precisely what
you want • How adjectives work • Making comparisons
• Saying *better* **64**

Review 2 **74**

8 **Vous aimez le sport?** *Do you like sport?*
Asking and saying what you do as a hobby • Likes and
dislikes • More negatives • When to use **savoir**; when
to use **connaître**: *to know* • What's the weather like? **76**

9 **Qu'est-ce qu'il faut faire?** *What should I do?*
Asking for assistance • Two very useful verbs: *to be able,
to want* • Giving and understanding instructions **86**

10 **À l'avenir** *In the future*
Name of the seasons • Saying what you usually do
using some reflexive verbs • Saying what you need
• Stating your intentions • The pronoun **y**: *there*
• Using capital letters • When to use **visiter** (*to visit*)
• Two useful verbs: **sortir** *to go out* and **venir** *to come* **96**

Review 3 **108**

11 **Les courses** *Shopping*
Shops in France • Food shopping • At the market
• Shopping for other things • In a clothes shop **112**

12 **Se reposer, dormir** *Resting, sleeping*
Choice of hotels • Looking for a hotel • In the hotel
• Complaining • The French alphabet • Booking online
• Sending an email **122**

13 **Bien manger, bien boire** *Eating and drinking well*
Eating out • Ordering a snack • At the restaurant   **132**

14 **Les transports publics** *Public transport*
Getting round Paris • Taking a taxi • Travelling by bus
• French railways • At the information office   **142**

15 **Faire du tourisme** *Sightseeing*
Planning a visit • At the Tourist Office • Museums
• Going on an excursion   **152**

16 **Sortir** *Going out*
Where to go • Booking a ticket • Booking a tennis court **162**

17 **L'argent** *Money*
Coins and banknotes in euros • Getting small change
• Changing money • An error in the bill   **172**

18 **Savoir faire face** *Troubleshooting*
Chemists in France • Medical treatment
• At the doctor's • At the police station   **180**

Answer key   **190**

French–English vocabulary   **209**

Credits   **222**

Meet the author

Born and educated in France, Dr Catrine Carpenter used to teach French as a Senior Lecturer at Brighton University. Having taught for over 30 years, she has acquired a wide and comprehensive experience in teaching French to both learners and teachers of French, and in publishing a whole range of learning and teaching materials. These fall into two main categories: audio, visual and web-based material, and language courses. The first language course she produced was *Teach yourself Beginner's French*, published by Hodder & Stoughton; the other two focused on undergraduate students intending to spend a year at a French university, and specialists of French in higher education. By conducting research into language learners' strategies, Dr Carpenter has pioneered a wide range of innovative language learning and teaching approaches including projects based on email exchanges between French and British undergraduates.

Over the last 30 years, Dr Carpenter has accrued a wealth of experience in teaching learners between the ages of 5 and 70 in the UK, and also in France, Spain, India and Africa. More recently, she has been teaching under- and post-graduate students specializing in French studies, International Business, Management and Tourism, Engineering and Architecture. She has also taught members of the public on bespoke and short courses run by the University of Brighton. These have included business people, flight crews and other professionals.

However, out of all her teaching commitments, Dr Carpenter states that teaching beginners is the most rewarding for her, as she firmly believes that good foundations in learning a language pave the way to successful language acquisition.

How to use this book

Units 1–10

Study the first ten units in order; as you do so, you will find you are acquiring many useful language uses, but they are not grouped in any sort of topic area. They are based on what we call language functions, which are uses of language that can apply to a wide variety of situations.

Units 1–10 all open with a cultural reading in English and a **Vocabulary builder** page with thematic groupings of related words that can be studied together, as well as new expressions – words and expressions needed to understand the upcoming conversations or reading passages. You will often notice missing words in the Vocabulary builder. Look for patterns to help you complete the lists.

Each of the first ten units includes at least one conversation or a description by French characters of some aspects of their everyday life. It is important to listen to or read this material at least twice; work out the meaning for yourself as far as you can, but use the lists of key words and phrases to help you.

The symbol ∩ indicates that the recording is recommended for the following section.

The **Language discovery** asks you to think about one or more aspects of the grammar seen in the **Conversation**. (See below for more information about the learning approach known as the **Discovery method**.) The **Learn more** and **Go further** sections in these units explain how the French in the material you have just studied is put together.

The **Practice** sections give you the opportunity to try out the French that has been presented in the unit; each exercise focuses on listening, reading, writing and speaking. The **Answer key** is at the back of the book. If you have difficulty with an item, try solving the problem by looking again at the French before using the Answer key as a last resort. However, do check the Answer key when you've done each exercise – it is important to go back over material in areas where you are making errors, rather than carrying on regardless, which is bound to get you into trouble later!

If you find you are making a large number of errors, try taking things more slowly and practising the phrases more as you go through the material in the unit – don't try an exercise until you are pretty sure you have understood everything that precedes it. When using the recording, make frequent use of the pause button – it's good for your pronunciation and your memory to repeat phrases as often as possible.

Finally, in every unit there is a short test – **Test yourself** – which enables you to check whether you can now do some of the language tasks covered by that unit. The answers to these tests are also given in the Answer key. Always check your answers, and revise the unit until you can do it without errors before you go on to the next unit. A thorough understanding of everything in Unit 1 is essential for you to succeed in Unit 2, and so on.

The **French–English vocabulary** allows you to quickly access all the vocabulary that is presented in the course.

Units 11–18

The next eight units are based on broad topic areas. They can be taken in any order, which enables you to learn first how to cope with public transport (see Unit 14), if this is what you feel you need to tackle before anything else.

Try to use the book little and often, rather than for long stretches at a time. Leave it somewhere handy so that you can pick it up for just a few minutes to refresh your memory again with what you were looking at the time before. Above all, talk to other French speakers or learners, if at all possible; failing that, talk to yourself, to inanimate objects, to the imaginary characters in this book (warn your family and friends!). If you can find someone else to learn along with you, that is a great bonus.

Do *all* the exercises, and do them more than once. Make maximum use of the audio: play it as background, even when half your mind is on something else, as well as using it when you are actually studying. The main thing is to create a continuous French 'presence', so that what you are learning is always at the front of your mind, and not overlaid with the thousand and one preoccupations we all have in our daily lives.

The Discovery method – Learn to learn!

There are lots of philosophies and approaches to language learning, some practical, some quite unconventional, and far too many to list here. Perhaps you know of a few, or even have some techniques of your own. In this book we have incorporated the **Discovery method** of learning, a sort of DIY approach to language learning. What this means is that you will be encouraged throughout the course to engage your mind and figure out the language for yourself, through identifying patterns, understanding grammar concepts, noticing words that are similar to English, and more. This method promotes *language awareness*, a critical skill in acquiring a new language. As a result of your own efforts, you will be able to better retain what you have learned, use it with confidence, and, even better, apply those same skills to *continuing* to learn the language (or, indeed, another one) on your own after you've finished this book.

Everyone can succeed in learning a language – the key is to *know how to learn* it. Learning is more than just reading or memorizing grammar and vocabulary. It's about being an *active* learner, learning in real contexts, and, most importantly, *using* what you've learned in different situations. Simply put, if you **figure something out for yourself**, you're more likely to understand it. And when you use what you've learned, you're more likely to remember it.

And because many of the essential but (let's admit it!) dull details, such as grammar rules, are introduced through the **Discovery method**, you'll have more fun while learning. Soon, the language will start to make sense and you'll be relying on your own intuition to construct original sentences *independently*, not just listening and repeating.

Enjoy yourself!

To make your learning easier and more efficient, a system of icons indicates the actions you should take:

 Play the audio track

 Write and make notes

 Figure something out for yourself

 Reading passage

 Culture tip

 Speak French out loud (even if you're alone)

 Exercises coming up!

Check your French ability (no cheating)

Learn to learn

Be a successful language learner

1 MAKE A HABIT OUT OF LEARNING

Study a little every day, between 20 and 30 minutes if possible, rather than two to three hours in one session. **Give yourself short-term goals**, e.g. work out how long you'll spend on a particular unit and work within the time limit. This will help you to **create a study habit**, much in the same way you would a sport or music. You will need to concentrate, so try to **create an environment conducive to learning** which is calm and quiet and free from distractions. As you study, do not worry about your mistakes or the things you can't remember or understand. Languages settle differently in our brains, but gradually the language will become clearer as your brain starts to make new connections. Just **give yourself enough time** and you will succeed.

2 EXPAND YOUR LANGUAGE CONTACT

As part of your study habit try to take other opportunities to **expose yourself to the language**. As well as using this book you could try listening to radio and television or reading articles and blogs. Perhaps you could find information in French about a personal passion or hobby or even a news story that interests you. In time you'll find that your vocabulary and language recognition deepen and you'll become used to a range of writing and speaking styles.

3 VOCABULARY

▶ To organize your study of vocabulary, group new words under:
  a generic categories, e.g. *food*, *furniture*.
  b situations in which they occur, e.g. under *restaurant* you can write *waiter*, *table*, *menu*, *bill*.
  c functions, e.g. greetings, parting, thanks, apologizing.
▶ Say the words out loud as you read them.
▶ Write the words over and over again. Remember that if you want to keep lists on your smartphone or tablet you can usually switch the keyboard language to make sure you are able to include all accents and special characters.

- ▶ Listen to the audio several times.
- ▶ Cover up the English side of the vocabulary list and see if you remember the meaning of the word.
- ▶ Associate the words with similar sounding words in English, e.g. **parler** *(to speak)* with *parlour*, a room where people chat.
- ▶ Create flash cards, drawings and mind maps.
- ▶ Write words for objects around your house and stick them to objects.
- ▶ Pay attention to patterns in words, e.g. adding **bon** or **bonne** to the start of a word usually indicates a greeting, **bonjour, bonsoir, bonne nuit**.
- ▶ **Experiment with words.** Use the words that you learn in new contexts and find out if they are correct. For example, you learn in Unit 5 that **passe** means *go* in the context of time, e.g. **le week-end passe trop vite** *(the week-end goes too quickly)*. Experiment with **passe** in new contexts, e.g. **les vacances** *(the holidays)* **passent trop vite**; **la semaine** *(the week)* **passe**... Check the new phrases either in this book, a dictionary or with French speakers.

4 GRAMMAR

- ▶ To organize the study of grammar write your own grammar glossary and add new information and examples as you go along.
- ▶ **Experiment with grammar rules.** Sit back and reflect on the rules you learn. See how they compare with your own language or other languages you may already speak. Try to find out some rules on your own and be ready to spot the exceptions. By doing this you'll remember the rules better and get a feel for the language.
- ▶ Try to find examples of grammar in conversations or other articles.
- ▶ Keep a 'pattern bank' that organizes examples that can be listed under the structures you've learned.
- ▶ Use old vocabulary to practise new grammar structures.
- ▶ When you learn a new verb form, write the conjugation of several different verbs you know that follow the same pattern.

5 PRONUNCIATION

- ▶ When organizing the study of pronunciation keep a section of your notebook for pronunciation rules and practise those that trouble you.
- ▶ Repeat all of the conversations, line by line. Listen to yourself and try to mimic what you hear.
- ▶ Record yourself and compare yourself to a native speaker.
- ▶ Make a list of words that give you trouble and practise them.

- ▶ Study individual sounds, then full words.
- ▶ Don't forget, it's not just about pronouncing letters and words correctly, but using the right intonation. So, when practising words and sentences, mimic the rising and falling intonation of native speakers.

6 LISTENING AND READING

The conversations in this book include questions to help guide you in your understanding. But you can go further by following some of these tips.

- ▶ **Imagine the situation.** When listening to or reading the conversations, try to imagine where the scene is taking place and who the main characters are. Let your experience of the world help you guess the meaning of the conversation, e.g. if a conversation takes place in a snack bar you can predict the kind of vocabulary that will be used.
- ▶ **Concentrate on the main part.** When watching a foreign film you usually get the meaning of the whole story from a few individual shots. Understanding a foreign conversation or article is similar. Concentrate on the main parts to get the message and don't worry about individual words.
- ▶ **Guess the key words; if you cannot, ask or look them up.** When there are key words you don't understand, try to guess what they mean from the context. If you're listening to a French speaker and cannot get the gist of a whole passage because of one word or phrase, try to repeat that word with a questioning tone; the speaker will probably paraphrase it, giving you the chance to understand it. If for example you wanted to find out the meaning of the word **voyager** (*to travel*) you would ask **Que veut dire voyager?**

7 SPEAKING

Rehearse in French. As all language teachers will assure you, the successful learners are those students who overcome their inhibitions and get into situations where they must speak, write and listen to the language. Here are some useful tips to help you practise speaking French:

- ▶ Hold a conversation with yourself, using the conversations of the units as models and the structures you have learnt previously.
- ▶ After you have conducted a transaction with a salesperson, clerk or waiter in your own language, pretend that you have to do it in French, e.g. *buying groceries, ordering food, drinks* and so on.
- ▶ Look at objects around you and try to name them in French.
- ▶ Look at people around you and try to describe them in detail.
- ▶ Try to answer all of the questions in the book out loud.

- Say the dialogues out loud then try to replace sentences with ones that are true for you.
- Try to role-play different situations in the book.

8 LEARN FROM YOUR ERRORS

- Don't let errors interfere with getting your message across. Making errors is part of any normal learning process, but some people get so worried that they won't say anything unless they are sure it is correct. This leads to a vicious circle as the less they say, the less practice they get and the more mistakes they make.
- Note the seriousness of errors. Many errors are not serious as they do not affect the meaning; for example if you use the wrong article (**le** for **la**), wrong pronouns (**je l'achète** for **je les achète**) or wrong adjective ending (**blanc** for **blanche**). So concentrate on getting your message across and learn from your mistakes.

9 LEARN TO COPE WITH UNCERTAINTY

- **Don't over-use your dictionary.** When reading a text in the foreign language, don't be tempted to look up every word you don't know. Underline the words you do not understand and read the passage several times, concentrating on trying to get the gist of the passage. If after the third time there are still words which prevent you from getting the general meaning of the passage, look them up in the dictionary.
- **Don't panic if you don't understand.** If at some point you feel you don't understand what you are told, don't panic or give up listening. Either try and guess what is being said and keep following the conversation or, if you cannot, isolate the expression or words you haven't understood and have them explained to you. The speaker might paraphrase them and the conversation will carry on.
- **Keep talking.** The best way to improve your fluency in the foreign language is to talk every time you have the opportunity to do so: keep the conversations flowing and don't worry about the mistakes. If you get stuck for a particular word, don't let the conversation stop; paraphrase or replace the unknown word with one you do know, even if you have to simplify what you want to say. As a last resort use the word from your own language and pronounce it in the foreign accent.

Pronunciation guide

1 HOW TO SOUND FRENCH

00.01

Here are a few rules that will help you to sound French right from the beginning:

1 In French, unlike in most English words, it is the last part of the word that bears a heavy stress:

res-tau-**rant**,   o-**range**,   ca-**fé**,   té-lé-**phone**

2 French words that are spelt like English words are almost always pronounced differently:

pardon, important, parking, sandwich, ticket

3 In general, consonants at the end of a word such as **d g p s t x z,** and the letter **h,** are silent.

vou**s**   anglai**s**   nui**t**   dame**s**   messieur**s**   **h**ôtel

2 FRENCH SOUNDS

00.02

Here is the list of the **French vowels** with a rough English equivalent sound. You'll see that an accent on an **e** or an **o** changes the way the letter is pronounced.

Letter	Rough English sound	French example
a à	c**a**t	m**a**dame
e	1 **a**bove 2 b**e**st (before two consonants or x) 3 m**ay** (before z, r)	l**e** n**e** m**e**rci parl**ez**
é	m**ay**	caf**é**
è ê	p**ai**r	p**è**re f**ê**te
i î y	pol**i**ce	merc**i** d**î**ner typ**i**que
o	d**o**t	**o**live
u	a sound not found in English – first say **oo**, but then keeping the lips in that position try saying **ee**	**u**ne d**u**
ai	as **è ê** above	l**ai**t s'il vous pl**aî**t

Letter	Rough English sound	French example
ô au eau	pronounced as **o** but with rounded lips	h**ô**tel **au**tobus b**eau**coup
eu œu	sir	l**eu**r s**œu**r
oi	the **wa** sound at the beginning of **one**	bons**oi**r
ou	m**oo**	v**ou**s

00.03

Many **consonants** are similar to English, with a number of exceptions and variations:

Letter	Rough English sound	French example
ç	**s**it	**ç**a fran**ç**ais
ch	**sh**op	**ch**ic
g	lei**su**re (before **i**, **e**)	Bri**g**itte
gn	o**ni**on	co**gn**ac
h	not pronounced	**h**ôtel **h**ôpital
j	lei**su**re	**j**e bon**j**our
l ll	**ye**s (often when **i** precedes **l**, **ll**)	fi**ll**e travai**l**
qu	**c**are	**qu**estion
r	pronounced at the back of the throat with the tongue touching the bottom teeth	**r**at Pa**r**is
s	de**s**ert (between vowels)	mademoi**s**elle
t	(before **ion**) pa**ss**	atten**t**ion
th	**t**ea	**th**é
w	1 **w**hat 2 **v**an	**w**hisky **w**agon-restaurant

Here are the **nasal sounds** formed usually with vowels followed by **m** or **n**. Speak through your nose when you pronounce them and listen carefully to the recording.

Letter	Rough English sound	French example
ein im in ain	b**ang** (stop before the g)	fre**in** **im**portant v**in** tr**ain** **im**possible
en an	l**on**g (stop before the g)	**en**core J**ean** restaur**ant**
on	as above but with lips pushed forward	pard**on** **on** n**on**
un um	similar to **ein im in ain**	parf**um** **un**

3 HOW TO LINK THE SOUNDS TOGETHER

00.04

To make the words run more smoothly, the final consonants of words which are usually silent are sounded when the next word starts with a vowel or **h**, e.g. **très_important** (trayzimportan). This is called a liaison. In some cases, as above, liaisons are essential; in other cases they are optional. To help you recognize when the liaisons are essential they'll be indicated with a linking mark (_) in Units 1–10.

When making liaisons, all French people:

1 pronounce **s** and **x** like **z**: le**s**_oranges;   deu**x**_heures

2 pronounce **d** and **t** like *t*, but the **t** of **et** (*and*) is never sounded: le gran**d**_homme;   c'es**t**_ici; un   café e**t** une bière

3 link **n** in the nasal **un** when the next words starts with a vowel or a silent **h**: u**n**_enfant;   u**n**_hôtel

4 AND NOW PRACTISE...

00.05

Starting with **Paris** on the following map, go round anti-clockwise saying each of the 14 towns out loud. Pause after each town and check your pronunciation with the recording.

Useful expressions

SALUTATIONS *GREETINGS*

Bonjour, Monsieur.	*Good morning, Sir.*
Salut!	*Hi! (informal)*
Bon après-midi.	*Good afternoon.*
Bonsoir, Madame.	*Good evening, Madam.*
Bonne nuit.	*Goodnight.*
Au revoir, Mademoiselle.	*Goodbye, Miss.*
À bientôt.	*See you soon.*
À tout à l'heure.	*See you later.*

COURTOISIES *COURTESIES*

s'il vous plaît	*please (formal)*
s'il te plaît	*please (informal)*
merci	*thanks*
merci bien/beaucoup	*thanks a lot/thank you very much*
Comment_allez-vous?	*How are you? (formal)*
Comment ça va?	*How are you? (informal)*
Ça va bien?	*Is everything all right? (informal)*
Très bien, merci.	*Very well, thank you.*
Bien, et vous?	*I'm fine, how about you? (formal)*
Pas mal, et toi?	*Not bad, and you? (informal)*
Pardon, Monsieur.	*Pardon me, Sir. (to apologize, to interrupt)*
Excusez moi, Madame.	*Excuse me, Madam. (to apologize, to interrupt)*

QUESTIONS SIMPLES *SIMPLE QUESTIONS*

Qui...?	*Who...?*
Qu'est-ce que...?	*What...?*
Où est/sont...?	*Where is/are...?*
Quand...?	*When...?*
Pourquoi...?	*Why...?*
Comment...?	*How...?*
Combien...?	*How much/many...?*

PRESENTATIONS *INTRODUCTIONS*

Je m'appelle...	*My name is...*
J'ai vingt-cinq ans.	*I am twenty five.*
Je suis anglais/e	*I am English.*
Je suis étudiant/e.	*I am a student.*
Je suis de Bristol.	*I am from Bristol.*
Je parle un peu français.	*I speak a little French.*

EXPRIMER VOS GOÛTS *EXPRESS YOUR TASTES*

J'aime...	*I like...*
J'adore...	*I love...*
Je n'aime pas...	*I don't like...*
Je déteste...	*I hate...*

BONS SOUHAITS *GOOD WISHES*

Bon anniversaire.	*Happy birthday.*
Bonne année.	*Happy New Year.*
Meilleurs voeux de...	*Best wishes for...*
Bonne santé!	*To your good health!*
Santé!	*To your health! (toast)*
À la vôtre/tienne!	*And to yours! (formal/informal)*

CONVERSATION FILLERS

Euh...	*Er...*
Eh bien...	*Well...*
Voyons...	*Let's see...*
Ça alors!	*(astonishment)*
Alors ça!	*(indignation)*
Et alors?!	*(defiance)*
Zut alors!	*Drat!*

LES CHIFFRES *NUMBERS*

Numbers are presented in detail in Units 2–6.

0	**zéro**	21	**vingt et un**	70	**soixante-dix**
1	**un**	22	**vingt-deux**	71	**soixante et onze**
2	**deux**	23	**vingt-trois**	72	**soixante-douze,** etc.
3	**trois**	24	**vingt-quatre**	80	**quatre-vingts**
4	**quatre**	25	**vingt-cinq**	81	**quatre-vingt-un**
5	**cinq**	26	**vingt-six**	82	**quatre-vingt-deux,** etc.
6	**six**	27	**vingt-sept**	90	**quatre-vingt-dix**
7	**sept**	28	**vingt-huit**	91	**quatre-vingt-onze**
8	**huit**	29	**vingt-neuf**	92	**quatre-vingt-douze,** etc.
9	**neuf**	30	**trente**	100	**cent**
10	**dix**	31	**trente et un**	101	**cent un**
11	**onze**	32	**trente-deux,** etc.	102	**cent deux,** etc.
12	**douze**	40	**quarante**	200	**deux cents**
13	**treize**	41	**quarante et un**	210	**deux cent dix**
14	**quatorze**	42	**quarante-deux,** etc.	300	**trois cents**
15	**quinze**	50	**cinquante**	331	**trois cent trente et un**
16	**seize**	51	**cinquante et un**		
17	**dix-sept**	52	**cinquante-deux,** etc.		
18	**dix-huit**	60	**soixante**		
19	**dix-neuf**	61	**soixante et un**		
20	**vingt**	62	**soixante-deux,** etc.		

1,000	**mille**	1,000,000	**un million**
2,000	**deux mille**	2,000,000	**deux millions**

Bonjour
Hello

In this unit you will learn how to:
▶ *say 'hello' and 'goodbye'.*
▶ *exchange greetings.*
▶ *observe basic courtesies.*
▶ *ask people to speak more slowly.*

CEFR: (A1) *Can establish social contact using basic greetings, leave-taking and giving thanks expressions; can respond to suggestions and apologies; can ask how people are.*

Vous parlez français?

How much **français** (*French*) do you suppose you already know? Some 1,700 words are identical in **anglais** (*English*) and in French, though their pronunciation may be **différente** (different).

Many everyday words of French origin, like *petite, normal, village,* or *patience,* expressions such as *en masse* or *rendez-vous,* and song lyrics like *Frère Jacques* may already be part of your English vocabulary, so you're off to a good start.

Consider the expression RSVP. In written French, the letters SVP stand for **s'il vous plaît** (*if you please*) and are common shorthand in letters and text messages.

What do you think the letter 'r' in RSVP stands for?
a retourner (return)
b répondez (respond)

🎙 Vocabulary builder

01.01 **Look at the vocabulary and expressions and complete the missing English translations. Then listen to the words and repeat.**

SALUTATIONS *GREETINGS*

bonjour	*good morning/afternoon, hello*
bonsoir *(after 5.00 p.m.)*	*good evening*
bonne nuit *(when going to bed)*	_____
au revoir	_____
bonjour, Madame	*good morning, Madam*
bonjour, Mademoiselle	*good morning, Miss*
bonsoir, Monsieur	*good evening, Sir*
au revoir, Messieurs-dames	*goodbye, ladies and gentlemen*

NEW EXPRESSIONS

oui, merci	_____ *thank you*
merci beaucoup	_____ *very much*
s'il vous plaît	_____
d'accord	*OK*
pardon	*sorry (to apologize), excuse me (to interrupt)*
Comment ça va? ça va *(informal)*	*How are things? fine*
Comment vas-tu?	*How are you?*
Comment_allez-vous? *(formal)*	*How are you?*
Je vais bien et toi?	*I am well – how about you?*
(Très) bien merci.	*(Very) well, thank you.*
Et vous? (formal)	_____
moi aussi	*me too*
Vous parlez_anglais?	*Do you speak English?*
je regrette	*I'm sorry, no/I'm afraid I don't*
parlez plus lentement	*speak more slowly*

> When you see a linking mark '_' between two words, sound the last letter of the first word as though it were attached to the next word: **comment_allez-vous?**
> Can you find another example of linking in the expressions above?

Conversations

SAYING HELLO

 1 01.02 **Listen to the conversations between people meeting friends and acquaintances. Then answer the questions.**

a When Does Roger see Nathalie, in the afternoon or in the evening? How can you tell?

Jane	Bonjour, Messieurs-dames.
Michel	Bonjour, Mademoiselle.
Jane	Bonjour, Monsieur.
Roger	Bonsoir, Madame.
Nathalie	Bonsoir, Monsieur.
Roger	Comment ça va, Jane?
Jane	Très bien, et toi?
Roger	Moi aussi, ça va bien.
Rosine	Comment vas-tu?
Jane	Je vais très bien Rosine, et toi?
Mme Dubois	Comment_allez-vous, Monsieur Dubosse?
M. Dubosse	Très bien merci, et vous?
Mme Dubois	Très bien.

b Which greeting does Jane use to address a group of people?
c What does Rosine say to ask *How are you?*
d What about Madame Dubois?

SAYING GOODBYE

01.03

Michel	Au revoir, Madame et ... merci beaucoup.
Nathalie	Au revoir, Monsieur.

2 **Now listen to the conversations again one sentence at a time and repeat, trying to imitate the pronunciation of the speakers.**

WHEN THINGS GET DIFFICULT...

3 01.04 **Jane and Nathalie are speaking to a garçon, where do you think they are?**

Jane	Pardon, Monsieur, vous parlez_anglais?
Garçon	Ah, non, je regrette...
Garçon	Bonjour, Madame. Qu'est-ce que vous désirez?
Nathalie	Parlez plus lentement, s'il vous plaît.
Garçon	D'accord... Qu'est-ce que vous désirez?

4 **Now put this jumbled dialogue in order, starting with 1.**

> **Qu'est-ce que vous désirez?** (lit.) *What do you wish?* but used in a café it means *Can I help you?*

_____ **a** Bien merci. Et vous?

_____ **b** Bonjour. Comment ça va?

_____ **c** Moi aussi, ça va.

___1___ **d** Bonjour, Mr Dubosse.

5 **Complete the dialogues with the words and expressions you have learned in this unit.**

Pardon, Madame, vous _____ anglais?

Ah non, je _____.

Je vais _____, et toi?

Oui, _____ aussi, ça va très bien.

Pardon, Monsieur?

Oui, Madame. _____ vous désirez?

Language discovery

SIMPLE QUESTIONS

 Read the following sentence out loud: **Ça va bien.** How can you turn this sentence into a question without adding anything to it or changing the word order?

In French the simplest way of asking something is to raise your voice on the last syllable (part of a word):

Vous parlez_an**glais**?   Par**don**?   Ça va **bien**?

Now practise saying **pardon**? (to have something repeated) and **pardon** (to apologize or attract someone's attention).

REFUSING POLITELY IN FRENCH

If you want to refuse something in France, you can say **non merci** or **merci** on its own.

HOW TO BE COURTEOUS

It's polite in French to say **Monsieur, Madame, Mademoiselle** when you initiate a conversation with someone, particularly after short phrases like **oui, non, bonjour** or **merci**.

WHEN TO USE *TU* AND WHEN TO USE *VOUS*

The equivalent of *you* in French can be either **tu** (informal) or **vous**. French people use **tu** when speaking to children, teenagers, relations and close friends. They use **vous** in work and business situations or when speaking to senior or old people. **Vous** is also used to address a group of people to whom one might say **tu** individually. The best advice is to say **vous** until you are addressed as **tu** or asked to use the **tu** form: **on se tutoie?** *shall we call each other* **tu?**

For each of the following situations, decide if the French would use tu or vous?

When speaking to....	tu	vous
a a younger brother/sister	✓	
b a group of 10 year olds		
c one's closest friend		
d a store clerk		
e an elderly neighbour		

ⓘ Practice

1 A person at the bus stop asks you a question that you do not hear properly. What do you say? Choose a, b or c.

  a s'il vous plaît   **c** pardon?

  b non merci

2 How would you say *hello* or *good night* in the following situations? Remember to add **Monsieur, Madame, Mademoiselle.** Write your answer underneath each picture.

(a) _____   (b) _____   (c) _____

(d) _____   (e) _____   (f) _____

3 You're arriving late at a hotel one evening; greet the person behind the reception desk by choosing the right phrase in the box below.

  (Au revoir, Madame)   (Bonsoir, Monsieur)

  (Pardon?)   (Bonjour, Messieurs-dames)

4 You are staying the night with some friends. It's late and you decide to go to bed. You say:

  (Au revoir) (Comment ça va?) (Bonne nuit)

5 You meet up with a French-speaking colleague. How do you ask: *How are you?*

  C _ _ _ _ _ _ _ a v _ ?

  The answer is *Very well, thank you.* What is it in French?

  T _ _ _ b _ _ _ _ _ _ _ i.

6 Use the clues to complete the grid. When you've finished, the vertical word will be what you say if you step on someone's foot!

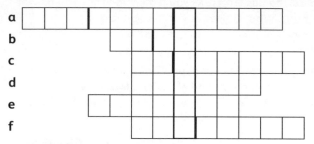

a The French translation for *please*.
b Your answer to a friend who asks how you are.
c *Goodbye*.
d Calling the waitress's attention.
e Greeting someone after 5 p.m.
f Refusing politely.

7 Choose the appropriate word or group of words.

a How would you greet several people?
1 Bonjour Madame.
2 Au revoir.
3 Bonjour Messieurs-dames.

b How would you refuse politely?
1 D'accord.
2 Non merci.
3 Pardon.

c To ask someone if s/he speaks English you say:
1 Parlez plus lentement.
2 Au revoir Messieurs-dames.
3 Vous parlez_anglais?.

d To wish someone good night you say:
1 Bonjour.
2 Bonsoir.
3 Bonne nuit.

e To express agreement with another person, you say:
1 Je regrette.
2 D'accord.
3 Très bien merci.

? Test yourself

1 **Complete the expressions with the correct word.**

   a bonne nuit/soir

   _____

   b ça va bon/bien

   _____

   c comment allez-/vas vous?

   _____

   d merci beaucoup/très bien.

   _____

2 **Put the words in order to make questions.**

   a bien / je / toi ? / vais / et

   _____

   b vous / qu'est-ce / désirez ? / que

   _____

   c allez / Monsieur ? / -vous, / comment

   _____

SELF CHECK	
I CAN. . .	
○	. . . say hello and goodbye.
○	. . . exchange greetings.
○	. . . accept and refuse politely.
○	. . . ask someone to speak more slowly.

C'est combien?
How much is it?

In this unit you will learn how to:
▶ *count up to ten.*
▶ *ask for something.*
▶ *ask the price.*

CEFR: (A1) *Can ask people for things; can handle numbers, quantities and costs.*

French café bars

For many French people, daily routine includes a stop at **le café du coin** (*the corner café*) to buy **le journal** (*the newspaper*), or **des timbres** (*some stamps*). Naturally, many French people frequent **le café du coin** to meet friends and have **une bière** (*a beer*) or **l'apéro** (*the aperitif*).

Traditionally, French cafés operated as **bars-tabac**, places to buy drinks as well as cigarettes. Nowadays, many supplement their income by offering meals or **des sandwiches** (*some sandwiches*), but you can trust the old **bar-tabac** sign to indicate an establishment that is part café, part **point-presse** (*newsagent*).

What words does French use to mean *the* and *some*? Such words are basic nuts and bolts of the language, and in this unit you get to learn how to use them.

🎙 Vocabulary builder

02.01 **Look at the words and complete the missing English equivalent. Then listen to the audio and imitate the French pronunciation.**

AU CAFÉ DU COIN *AT THE CORNER CAFÉ*

un café	_____
un thé	_____
une bière	*a beer*
l'eau minérale (f)	*the mineral/bottled water*
l'eau gazeuse/plate	*sparkling/still _____*
du vin	*some wine*
de la limonade	*some _____*
une bouteille	*one bottle*
du pain	*some bread*
une baguette	*a French stick*
des sandwiches	*some _____*
un_euro	*a euro*
le timbre	*the stamp*
la carte postale	*the _____*
l'addition (f)	*the bill*
les toilettes	*the _____*

NEW EXPRESSIONS

Je voudrais...	*I would like...*
Vous_avez...?	*Do you have...?*
ça	*this/that*
C'est combien?	*How much is it?*
Je n'en_ai pas.	*I haven't got any.*
Avec ça?	*Anything else?*
C'est tout?	*Is that all?*

02.02 **Listen to a French speaker counting to ten and pay close attention to the number seven. Which letter is not pronounced?**

1	un	2	deux	3	trois	4	quatre	5	cinq
6	six	7	sept	8	huit	9	neuf	10	dix

Conversation

*Jane is in **un magasin d'alimentation** (grocer's shop), asking for a few things.*

🎧 **1** 02.03 **Listen to the conversation first, then answer the questions.**
   a What does she want to buy?
   b Does she get what she wants?

Jane	Vous_avez de la bière?
Vendeuse	Ah non, je regrette, je n'en_ai pas.
Jane	Et du vin?
Vendeuse	Euh oui. Quel vin désirez-vous?
Jane	Je voudrais une bouteille de Muscadet.
Vendeuse	Oui, voilà... et avec ça?
Jane	Deux bouteilles d'eau minérale.
Vendeuse	De la gazeuse ou de la plate?
Jane	De la plate.
Vendeuse	Bon, très bien. C'est tout?
Jane	Oui, merci. C'est combien?
Vendeuse	Pour le Muscadet, c'est 6€50 et pour l'eau minérale, 1€ 30 la bouteille.

2 **Find the expressions in the conversation that mean:**
   a two bottles of water
   b Is that all?
   c How much is it?

la vendeuse	*the shop assistant (female)*
Quel vin?	*Which wine?*
voilà	*there you are*
six_euros cinquante	*6€ 50*
un_euro trente	*1€ 30*

HOW TO PRONOUNCE *SIX* AND *DIX*

▶ When **six** and **dix** are on their own as numbers the **x** is pronounced as **s** and they rhyme with 'peace': **vous_avez des timbres? Oui, six.**

▶ When followed by a word starting with a consonant the **x** is not pronounced and they sound like 'dee' and 'see': **dix kilos, six bières.**

▶ When followed by a word starting with a vowel or **h** pronounce the **x** and **s** as **z**: **six_euros, dix_hôtels.**

Language discovery

1 WORDS FOR 'A', 'AN': *UN, UNE*

The word *a* or *an* is **un** in front of a masculine noun and **une** in front of a feminine noun. All French nouns belong to one of the two groups: masculine or feminine. Sometimes it is obvious as in **un Français** *a Frenchman*, **une Française** *a Frenchwoman*, while at other times it is not obvious as in **un café** but **une bière**.

2 WORDS FOR 'THE': *LE, LA, L', LES*

Look at the last line of the conversation: **Pour *le muscadet*, pour *l'eau minérale*, ... pour *la bouteille*. How would you translate the words in italics?**

There are four different ways of saying *the*:

le with masculine nouns	**le timbre**
la with feminine nouns	**la gare**
l' with nouns starting with a vowel or an **h**	**l'hôtel (m) l'eau (f)**
les with plural nouns	**les toilettes**

Plural nouns usually take an **s** at the end. Make a habit of learning words together with **le** or **la** before them. If they start with a vowel or **h**, they are followed by (m) or (f) in the French–English vocabulary to indicate whether they are masculine or feminine.

3 WORDS FOR 'SOME', 'ANY': *DU, DE LA, DE L', DES*

When **de** (*of*) is used in combination with **le**, **la**, **l'**, **les** it changes its form and can mean *some* or *any* according to the context:

de + le becomes **du**   **de l'** remains unchanged

de la remains unchanged   **de + les** becomes **des**

Compare the examples below:

Je voudrais **du** vin.	*I would like some wine.*
Je voudrais **le** vin.	*I would like the wine.*
Vous_avez **de la** bière?	*Do you have any beer?*
Vous_avez **la** bière?	*Do you have the beer?*
Vous_avez **de l'**eau minérale?	*Have you any mineral water?*
Vous_avez **l'**eau minérale?	*Do you have the mineral water?*
Je voudrais **des** timbres.	*I would like some stamps.*
Je voudrais **les** timbres.	*I would like the stamps.*

In English we often omit the word **some**. In French, **de** + the definite article (**le**, **la**, **l'** or **les**) is almost always used.

4 UN/UNE

To ask for one of something use **un** with masculine nouns and **une** with feminine nouns:

un timbre	*one postage stamp*
une eau gazeuse	*one sparkling water*

5 C'EST COMBIEN? *HOW MUCH IS IT?*

You need only two words to ask for the price: **C'est combien?** *How much is it?* followed by whatever you want to know the price of:

C'est combien la carte postale?	*How much is the postcard?*
C'est combien la baguette?	*How much is the French stick?*

You will come across **C'est** a lot more in the next few units. It is a useful word which can mean any of the following: *he is, she is, it is.*

🔓 Practice

1 **Look at the objects below, and write their names in French preceded by *un*, *une* or *des*.**

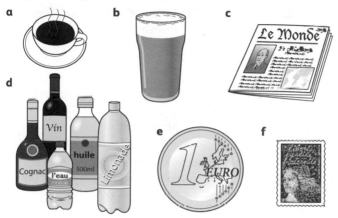

a
b
c
d
e
f

2 **You're sitting in a French café; you want to ask for three things. What are they? You will find them hidden in the string of letters below:**

MotlestoilettespozowiuncafémoghtLluddItiondfc

3 **Before going back to your hotel, you want to buy a few things: how would you ask for them In French?**

    a I would like four postcards, please.

    _____

    b Do you have four stamps for England?

    _____ pour l'Angleterre?

    c And some aspirin, please.

    et _____

    d How much is it?

    _____

4 **Unscramble the words to make sentences.**

    a c'est / la / d'eau? / combien / bouteille

    b voudrais / une / je / limonade

    c sandwiches? / avez / des / vous

    d c'est / trente / euro / un

Listen and understand

 Michel, sitting at a café, is ordering some drinks with his friends.
He then asks for the bill.

1 02.04 **Complete the dialogue with the words in the box. Then listen to the audio and check your answers.**

café	voudrais	addition	Messieurs-dames	bière

Garçon   Bonjour, (a) _____

Michel   Je voudrais_un (b) _____ et vous, Marie?

Marie   Moi, une (c) _____.

Sylvie   Je (d) _____ une limonade.

Michel   Et je voudrais aussi l' (e) _____, s'il vous plaît.

2 02.05 **As numbers are very important, here's another chance to practise them. Write your answers to the following sums (in words, not figures).**

a deux + trois = _____

b cinq + quatre = _____

c neuf + un = _____

d six + trois = _____

e dix − huit = _____

f sept − trois = _____

g trois × trois = _____

h quatre × deux = _____

Check your answers by listening to the audio, or look them up in the Answer key.

Test yourself

1 **Match the words in the left-hand column with the ones on the right.**

a	Je voudrais	1	du pain?
b	une bouteille	2	l'addition, s'il vous plaît.
c	Vous avez	3	le thé?
d	C'est combien	4	d'eau plate

2 **All the numbers from one to ten are listed in French in this wordsearch except for one. Which is missing? Read horizontally or vertically, either forwards or backwards.**

E	Y	Q	N	I	C
R	S	E	P	T	R
T	M	I	D	I	X
A	O	N	E	U	F
U	L	U	U	H	I
Q	S	H	X	I	S

You'll find the answers to Test yourself in the Answer key at the end of the book. If they are correct you are ready to move to Unit 3. If you found the test difficult, spend more time revising Unit 2.

SELF CHECK

	I CAN...
○	. . . count from 1 to 10.
○	. . . ask for things at a café or in a shop.
○	. . . ask the price of things.

3 Je m'appelle ...
Et vous?

My name is ... What's yours?

In this unit you will learn how to:
▶ *count up to 20.*
▶ *talk about yourself and your family.*
▶ *say that things are not so.*
▶ *say how old you are.*

CEFR: (A1) *Can ask and answer questions about personal details such as nationality and where people live or are from; can use phrases and sentences to describe family and other people.*

Family ties

It's likely that your first conversations in French will be about your **famille** (*family*). You can expect questions about your close family, your **mère et père** (*mother and father*) or your **frères et soeurs** (*brothers and sisters*). You may also be asked about your relationships and if you are **marié/e** (*married*), if you have **des enfants** (*children*) and if they are **un garçon** (*a boy*) or **une fille** (*a girl*).

The verbs **avoir** (*to have*) and **être** (*to be*) are two of the most useful verbs in French and a main topic of this unit. Practise using them until they become automatic and you can use them without thinking. Good command of these verbs can make all the difference in understanding what the French mean.

Can you figure out the difference between these two sentences?
Je suis une fille, and **j'ai une fille.** Look at the Vocabulary builder to check your intuition.

Vocabulary builder

03.01 **Look at the words and complete the missing English expressions. Then listen to the audio and imitate the French pronunciation.**

LA FAMILLE *THE FAMILY*

la fille/le fils	*daughter/son*
la sœur/le frère	*sister/ _____*
le père/la mère	*_ _____ /mother*
les parents/les grands-parents	*parents/ _____*
le grand-père/la grand-mère	*grandfather/ _____*
un copain/petit_ami	*a boyfriend*
une copine/petite amie	*_____*
une fille et un garçon	*a girl and a boy*

NEW EXPRESSIONS

Je m'appelle ... et toi/vous?	*My name is ... what's yours? (informal/formal)?*
Tu es français?	*Are you French? (informal/man)*
Vous_êtes française?	*(formal/woman)*
Je suis_anglais/anglaise.	*I'm English. (man/woman)*
Tu es marié?	*Are you married? (informal/man)*
Vous_êtes mariée?	*(formal/woman)*
Non, je ne suis pas marié.	*No, I am not married.*
Je suis divorcé/e.	*I am divorced. (man/woman)*
Vous_avez des_enfants?	*Do you have any children?*
Ils_ont dix et six ans.	*They are ten and six years old.*
Non, je n'ai pas d'enfants.	*No, I have no children.*
J'habite en_Angleterre.	*I live/I'm living in England.*
avec ma famille	*with my family*
Je travaille à New York.	*I work in New York.*
Je viens/suis de Vancouver.	*I am/come from Vancouver.*
Elle est secrétaire/comptable.	*She is a secretary/an accountant.*
Elle travaille dans une banque.	*She works in a bank.*
Il travaille pour IBM.	*He works for IBM.*
à mi-temps/à temps plein	*part-time/full-time*

In English *a* is used before a profession. In French it is always omitted: **Elle est professeure.** *She is a teacher.*

Conversation

Jane is sitting on the terrace of a café reading an English magazine.
A Frenchwoman has struck up a conversation with her.

1 03.02 **Listen to the conversation, then answer the questions.**

   a Do both women work?

Frenchwoman	Vous_êtes_anglaise?
Jane	Je suis_anglaise et irlandaise. J'ai un père anglais et une mère irlandaise.
Frenchwoman	Ah c'est bien. Et vous_habitez Londres?
Jane	Non. Je suis de Londres, mais j'habite Brighton.
Frenchwoman	C'est où ça, Brighton?
Jane	Dans le sud de l'Angleterre. Et vous, vous_êtes française?
Frenchwoman	Oui, je suis de Lille dans le nord de la France, mais j'habite Paris avec ma famille.
Jane	Vous_êtes mariée?
Frenchwoman	Divorcée, mais je vis_avec un copain depuis cinq ans.
Jane	Et vous_avez des_enfants?
Frenchwoman	Oui, j'ai trois_enfants, une fille et deux garçons.
Jane	Ils_ont quel âge?
Frenchwoman	La fille a dix_ans et les garçons ont huit_ans et six_ans.
Jane	Ah, très bien.
Frenchwoman	Et vous, vous_êtes mariée?
Jane	Non, je ne suis pas mariée, mais moi aussi j'ai un petit_ami.
Frenchwoman	Il est_anglais?
Jane	Non, il est_américain. Il travaille pour IBM en Angleterre.
Frenchwoman	Ah c'est bien. Et vous, vous travaillez?
Jane	Oui, je suis dentiste.
Frenchwoman	Moi aussi, je travaille à mi-temps dans_une agence de voyages.
Jane	C'est bien votre travail?
Frenchwoman	Oui, très. Je parle beaucoup anglais avec les touristes. Mais vous, vous parlez très bien français.
Jane	Non, seulement un petit peu ...

   b What is Jane's nationality?
   c Has she got any children?
   d Is Jane married?
   e What is her job?

irlandais/e	*Irish*
Je vis ...	*I have been living ...*
depuis cinq ans.	*for five years.*
moi aussi	*me too*
une agence de voyages	*a travel agency*
seulement un petit peu	*only a little*

2 **How much have you understood? Decide if the following sentences are (T) true or (F) false.**

   a Jane lives in Brighton.

   b The Frenchwoman's family lives in Lille.

   c Jane is not in a relationship.

   d The Frenchwoman compliments Jane on her spoken French.

Pronunciation

▶ **nom** (*name*) is pronounced like **non** (*no*).

▶ **fille** Is pronounced 'fee-ye' and **fils** is pronounced 'fee-sse'.

▶ Some liaisons are essential, others are optional. For example, in the question **vous_avez des_enfants?** both liaisons are essential. In **vous_êtes_anglais?** you need to link **vous_êtes** but you can say either **êtes_anglais** or **êtes anglais**. Today the French tend to drop their liaisons.

Look at the Vocabulary builder section and try to practise linking the words with a linking mark, e.g. **vous_êtes** (pronounce 'vou zêtes').

Language discovery

1 REGULAR VERBS ENDING IN -*ER*, **E.G.** *PARLER,* **'TO SPEAK'**

In English *to speak* is the infinitive of the verb (this is the form of the verbs you find in the dictionary). In French the equivalent infinitive is **parler**. It follows the same pattern as many other verbs with infinitives ending in **-er**. Here is the present tense of **parler**:

	parler	*to speak*
je	par**le**	*I speak, I'm speaking*
tu	par**les**	*you speak, you're speaking*
il/elle/on	par**le**	*he/she/one speaks, is speaking*
nous	par**lons**	*we speak, we're speaking*
vous	par**lez**	*you speak, you're speaking*
ils/elles	par**lent**	*they speak, they're speaking*

▶ The present tense in French makes no distinction between *I speak* and *I'm speaking*.

▶ Before a vowel or **h**, **je** becomes **j'**: **j'habite** *I live*.

▶ **On** is commonly used in French when people talk about themselves. In a general sense it is the equivalent of *one, you, we*. **On habite Paris.**

▶ **Ils** is used when the group of people is mixed or includes only males.

▶ **Elles** is for an all-female group.

▶ Pronunciation: the **je, tu, il, elle, on, ils, elles** forms of the present tense of any regular **-er** verb sound the same. Do not pronounce the third person plural ending **-ent**. If you do, people may not understand you.

 Can you work out the present tense of *travailler*? Write it down and read it out loud. Remember the pronunciation tips above.

---

2 TWO IMPORTANT VERBS: *AVOIR* 'TO HAVE', *ÊTRE* 'TO BE'

Avoir and **être** are irregular, i.e. they do not follow the normal pattern. They are the two most common verbs in French and need to be learnt individually:

avoir	*to have*	être	*to be*
j'ai	*I have*	**je suis**	*I am*
tu as	*you have*	**tu es**	*you are*
il/elle/on_a	*he/she/one has*	**il/elle/on_est**	*he/she/one is*
nous_avons	*we have*	**nous sommes**	*we are*
vous_avez	*you are*	**vous_êtes**	*you are*
ils/elles_ont	*they have*	**ils/elles sont**	*they are*

Pratiquez! Practise the verbs **avoir** and **être** in sentences using the words you already know. Remember that for a question, you need to raise the voice on the last syllable. For example:

J'**ai** un_enfant.

Tu **as** des_enfants?

Il **a** trois frères.

Nous_**avons**...

Je **suis** marié.

Tu **es**_anglaise?

Elle **est** professeure.

3 THE NEGATIVE FORM: *NE ... PAS*

To say something is not so in French, you put **ne**... **pas** round the verb.

Je **ne** comprends **pas.**   *I don't understand.*

Ne becomes **n'** if the following verb starts with a vowel or **h**.

Je **n'**habite **pas** Paris.   *I don't live in Paris.*

> Today **ne** is often omitted in French conversations: **Je parle pas anglais.**

4 NUMBERS 11–20

🎧 03.03

11	**onze**	16	**seize**
12	**douze**	17	**dix-sept**
13	**treize**	18	**dix-huit**
14	**quatorze**	19	**dix-neuf**
15	**quinze**	20	**vingt** (pronounced as French **vin**)

💡 Contrast the numbers 17, 18 and 19. Refer back to the section How to Pronounce *six* and *dix* and find out which of the three numbers does not follow the rule?

5 ADJECTIVES: HOW THEY AGREE

To describe things in detail or talk about yourself you need to add descriptive words (called adjectives) to nouns. As a general rule, feminine adjectives end in **-e** and the plural adjectives take an **-s**, but it is not pronounced:

J'ai un_ami **américain.**	*I have an American friend.*
J'ai une amie **américaine.**	*I have an American friend.*
Mes_amis sont_ **américains.**	*My friends are American.*

6 CAPITAL LETTERS

In French, adjectives of nationality and names of languages are not written with a capital letter (unless they start a sentence):

Vous parlez **français?**	*Do you speak French?*
Je suis **canadien.**	*I am Canadian.*

but:

un(e) Anglais(e)	*an Englishman/woman*
un(e) Américain(e)	*an American*
un(e) Français(e)	*a Frenchman/woman*

7 SAYING HOW OLD YOU ARE

Start with **j'ai** (not **je suis**), add your age followed by **ans** (*years*):

Vous_avez quel âge?	*How old are you?*
J'ai dix-sept ans.	*I am 17.*

🔓 Practice

🎧 **1** 03.04 **On the audio you will hear some numbers between 1 and 20. Repeat and write them down in figures.**

a _____   f _____

b _____   g _____

c _____   h _____

d _____   i _____

e _____   j _____

2 **This time practise these sums out loud and write the answers in words. (+ is plus in French and – is moins.)**

a $10 + 3 =$ d $19 - 8 =$

b $15 + 5 =$ e $16 - 10 =$

c $13 + 6 =$ f $15 - 3 =$

3 **You are being very negative and answer non ... to all the following questions using ne ... pas:**

a Il est marié? Non, il _____ .

b Elle est secrétaire? Non, elle _____ .

c Ils_ont des enfants? Non, ils _____ .

d Brighton est dans le nord de l'Angleterre? Non, Brighton _____ .

e Vous parlez français? Non, je _____ .

f Il a 18 ans? Non, il _____ .

2 **Look at the family tree and complete the sentences.**

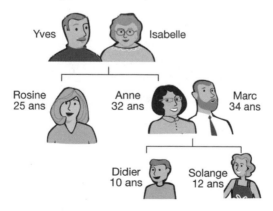

a Isabelle _____ mariée avec Yves.
b Ils _____ deux filles.
c _____ s'appellent Rosine et Anne.
d Anne et Marc ont deux _____, une fille et _____ fils.
e Rosine _____ _____ d'enfants.
f Elle _____ _____ mariée.
g Didier est le _____ de Solange.
h Solange _____ la sœur de Didier.

Reading

1 03.05 **Read along as you listen to the passage on la famille Guise. Look back at the family tree in Activity 4 to help you. Then answer the questions.**

LA FAMILLE GUISE

> Monsieur et Madame Guise sont français. Ils_ habitent Chaville, 15 rue de la Gare et ils travaillent à Paris. Yves est **comptable** et Isabelle travaille dans la **publicité**. Monsieur et Madame Guise ne parlent pas anglais. Ils_ont deux filles: Rosine qui a vingt-cinq ans et Anne qui a trente-deux_ans. Rosine travaille dans_une banque, elle est divorcée. Anne est **secrétaire** et travaille à mi-temps. Elle est mariée avec Marc qui est professeur de math dans_une école. Ils_ont deux_enfants: une fille, Solange, et un fils, Didier. Solange a douze_ans, Didier a dix_ans. Anne et Marc parlent anglais tous les deux.

a What is Yves' job?
b Where does Isabelle work?
c Who works part-time?

🔲 Test yourself

1 What is the French for the following questions?

a Are you working? (formal)

_____

b Are you married ? (man)

_____

c Do you have children ? (formal)

_____

d How old are they ?

_____

2 Match the questions and the answers.

a Tu parles anglais?   1 Oui, j'habite Paris.
b Et vous, vous travaillez?   2 Non, je suis canadien.
c Vous_êtes irlandais?   3 Oui, je suis comptable.
d Vous_habitez en France?   4 Oui, je parle anglais.

3 Make these sentences feminine.

a Il est américain.

_____

b Tu n'as pas un ami anglais.

_____

c Il est marié.

_____

d Ils travaillent dans une agence de voyages.

_____

SELF CHECK

I CAN. . .
○ . . . count up to 20
○ . . . talk about myself and my family.
○ . . . say that things are not so.
○ . . . say people's ages.

R1 Review 1

This Review contains a series of short tasks which use the main vocabulary and phrases, skills and language points in Units 1–3. We indicate the number of points allocated to each answer, so that you can keep your own score (out of a total of 40 points).

1 Match the words from each column to make sentences.

a	Tu	1	habitent Bordeaux.
b	Elle	2	êtes divorcé.
c	Nous	3	parle lentement.
d	Vous	4	sommes mariés.
e	Ils	5	parles très bien anglais.

Points: __ /5

2 Work out the sums, then write out the number in French.

a $9 + 3 =$

b $6 + 3 =$

c $17 - 4 =$

d $10 + 8 =$

e $16 - 2 =$

Points: __ /5

3 Make these sentences formal. Use vous.

a Et toi, tu travailles dans une banque?

b Tu as des_enfants?

c Tu es mariée?

d Tu parles français et anglais, non?

e Répète, s'il te plaît.

Points: __ /5

4 Complete the text with the right endings of the verbs avoir (to have) or être (to be).

Je **(a)** _____ anglais e et française, mais ma mère **(b)** _____ française. Mon père et ma mère **(c)** _____ mariés depuis 50 ans. J' **(d)** _____ trois frères qui ne **(e)** _____ pas mariés et une sœur qui **(f)** _____ deux enfants. Ils **(g)** _____ quinze et dix ans. Ma sœur et moi **(h)** _____ un mari anglais et nous **(i)** _____ professeures de français en Angleterre. Je n' **(j)** _____ pas d'enfants.

Points: __ /10

5 Make these sentences negative.

a Je comprends.

b Elle a de la bière.

c Vous habitez Londres.

d Ils_ont trois enfants.

e Elle est professeure.

Points: __ /5

6 If these are the answers, what were the questions?

a Je vais bien, et vous?

b Oui, ils_habitent Paris.

c Je m'appelle Morgane Dufour.

d Non, je ne suis pas français. Je suis allemand.

e Oui, je parle un peu anglais.

f Non, nous n'avons pas d'enfants.

g Je suis_étudiante, mais je travaille dans un cinéma.

h Oui, elle est mariée avec Martin.

i C'est 1 €05 la baguette de pain.

j J'ai vingt_ans. Et toi?

Points: __ /10

TOTAL __ /40

You will find the answers to the test questions in the Answer key to the exercises and tests Here are a few guidelines to help you grade your performance:

35–40 points	*Congratulations! You are ready to start Unit 4.*
25–34 points	*Very good. You have good control of the language covered so far. Try to identify your weak points and practise them again.*
20–24 points	*Well done, but look at your detailed scores and revise before moving on to Unit 4.*
19 points or less	*Not bad, but you will need to go back over the first three units. When you feel ready, take the test again and see how much you have improved.*

Vous habitez où?

Where do you live?

In this unit you will learn...
- *numbers from 20 to 70.*
- *simple and useful questions.*
- *how to say that things are yours or someone else's.*
- *how to understand prices.*

CEFR: (A1) *can handle numbers, can ask and answer practical wh-, do ... and is there/are there ... questions, can give and receive information about prices*

Suburban life

With 2.2 million inhabitants, Paris is a relatively small capital city. But if you add **les banlieues** (*the suburbs*), the greater Paris area is home to 11 million, or nearly one in every six French people.

Les banlieues are independent **villes** (*towns*) with **des trains directs** (*direct trains*) to the centre of Paris. Many **hommes et femmes d'affaires** (*businessmen and women*) commute long distances in order to enjoy **la vie de banlieue** (suburban life) and be able to go places **à pied** (*on foot*) once they get home.

Access and transport costs are important concerns for suburbanites, so you need to be able to ask the right questions: **c'est loin, la gare?** (*how far is the station?*), or **c'est combien, le billet?** (*how much is the ticket?*).

What French words from the text mean *men and women*?
Can you guess the meaning of this sentence? **Vous_habitez à Paris ou dans la banlieue?**

Vocabulary builder

04.01 **Listen to the questions and answers in Comment demander simplement. Pay attention to the speakers' intonation as you do. Make sure that you can you tell the difference between the questions and the answers.**

COMMENT DEMANDER SIMPLEMENT... *HOW TO ASK SIMPLY...*

C'est loin, la gare?	*How far is the station?*
C'est_au bout de la rue.	*It is at the end of the street.*
C'est près d'ici.	*It is nearby.*
C'est_à 50 mètres d'ici.	*It is 50 metres away (lit. 50 m from here).*
C'est_à cinq minutes à pied.	*It is five minutes away on foot.*
C'est_une grande ville.	*It is a big town.*
C'est_une petite piscine.	*It is a small swimming pool.*
C'est combien, le billet?	*How much is the ticket?*
C'est où, l'arrêt d'autobus?	*Where is the bus stop?*
C'est où, la station de métro?	*Where is the tube (subway) station?*
C'est quand, le départ?	*When is the departure?*
C'est cher/bon marché?	*Is it expensive/cheap?*

NEW EXPRESSIONS

Vous vous_appelez comment?	*What's your name?*
Je m'appelle...	*My name is...*
Le magasin est_ouvert?	*Is the shop open?*
Non, il est fermé.	*No, it's closed.*
Il y a un train direct pour Paris?	*Is there a direct train to Paris?*
Oui, il y en_a un.	*Yes, there is one.*
Il y a beaucoup de...	*There are a lot of...*

Look at the vocabulary again and find all the pairs of opposite words. (There are four, we have given you one.) One way to retain more vocabulary is to learn words in pairs with their opposites.

a _____

b _____

c cher/bon marché

d _____

Conversation

Jane has been invited to an office party. She gets to know Mr Durand, one of her friend's colleagues.

🎧 04.02 **Listen to the conversation, then answer the questions.**

    a Does Jean Durand live near Paris?

Jane	Vous vous_appelez comment?
Jean Durand	Je m'appelle Jean Durand et vous?
Jane	Moi, Jane Wilson. Vous_habitez où?
Jean Durand	Dans la banlieue de Paris, à Chatou.
Jane	Et ... c'est loin Chatou?
Jean Durand	C'est_à 45 minutes en train. Il y a un train direct Paris–Chatou.
Jane	Et ... vous travaillez?
Jean Durand	Oui, je suis_homme d'affaires et vous?
Jane	Moi, je travaille en_Angleterre, à Brighton ... je suis dentiste.
Jean Durand	Et vous_êtes_en vacances?
Jane	Oui, je suis_ici depuis deux semaines. J'aime beaucoup Paris. Vous_êtes marié?
Jean Durand	Oui.
Jane	Vous_avez des_enfants?
Jean Durand	J'ai trois_enfants: deux filles et un garçon.
Jane	Il y a une école à Chatou?
Jean Durand	Oui. Il y en_a une à dix minutes à pied.
Jane	Votre femme travaille?
Jean Durand	Oui, elle est professeure à l'école de Chatou.
Jane	C'est_une grande ville, Chatou?
Jean Durand	Oui, c'est grand. Il y a beaucoup de magasins, deux banques, une pharmacie, un parc et une piscine.

    b How many children does he have?

    c What does his wife do?

    d What about Jane, is she working in France?

quarante-cinq	*45*
en vacances	*on holiday*
depuis deux semaines	*for two weeks*
j'aime	*I like/love*
une école	*a school*
votre femme	*your wife*
un parc	*a park*

Language discovery

1 HOW TO ASK SIMPLE QUESTIONS

As you already know, the easiest way to ask a question is to make a statement and raise the voice on the word or the last syllable:

Vous_habitez où? *Where do you live?*

2 C'EST...? *IS IT...? IS THAT...?*

You can start the question with **c'est** (*it is*) and raise the voice at the end of the sentence. To say that it isn't use **ce n'est pas**:

C'est loin? *Is is far?*

Non, ce n'est pas loin. *No, it isn't far.*

3 IL Y A...? *IS THERE...? ARE THERE...?*

You can also start the question with **Il y a** (*there is, there are*) and raise the voice at the end of the sentence. To say *there is no...* or *there are no...*, use **il n'y a pas de...**

Il y a un restaurant dans l'hôtel? *Is there a restaurant in the hotel?*

Non, il n'y a pas de restaurant ici. *No, there is no restaurant here.*

 Pratiquez! *Practise!* **Il y a** and **c'est** are two easy French phrases which you can often start a question with. How would you ask the following:

_____ une pharmacie à Chatou?

_____ loin le cinéma?

4 OTHER QUESTIONS

You can form other questions starting with **c'est** or giving a statement and adding the question word afterwards:

C'est combien, le billet?	*How much is the ticket?*
C'est où, l'arrêt d'autobus?	*Where is the bus stop?*
C'est quand, les vacances?	*When are the holidays?*
C'est quoi le nom de l'hôtel?	*What's the name of the hotel?*
Les magasins ferment quand?	*When do the shops shut?*
Les magasins ouvrent quand?	*When do the shops open?*

5 MON, TON, SON *MY, YOUR, HIS*

thing possessed	my	your	his/her/ its/one's		our	your	their
masc. sing.	mon	ton	son		notre	votre	leur
fem. sing.	ma	ta	sa		notre	votre	leur
masc. & fem. pl.	mes	tes	ses		nos	vos	leurs

Like all adjectives in French, these agree with the noun they refer to:

mon mari   *my husband*

ma femme   *my wife*

mes enfants   *my children*

Take care when using **son** and **sa** to make them agree with the thing being owned, and not the owner:

le fils de M. Durand becomes **son fils** (*his son*)

le fils de Mme Durand becomes **son fils** (*her son*)

la fille de M. Durand becomes **sa fille** (*his daughter*)

la fille de Mme Durand becomes **sa fille** (*her daughter*)

Go further

NUMBERS 20–70

04.03 **Listen and read the pronunciation note, then practise saying the numbers.**

20 **vingt**	28 **vingt-huit**	50 **cinquante**
21 **vingt_et un**	29 **vingt-neuf**	51 **cinquante et un**
22 **vingt-deux**	30 **trente**	52 **cinquante-deux**
23 **vingt-trois**	31 **trente et un**	60 **soixante**
24 **vingt-quatre**	32 **trente-deux**	61 **soixante et un**
25 **vingt-cinq**	40 **quarante**	62 **soixante-deux**
26 **vingt-six**	41 **quarante et un**	70 **soixante-dix**
27 **vingt-sept**	42 **quarante-deux**	

Notice how for 21, 31, 41, 51, 61, one says **vingt_et un** (*twenty and one*), **trente_et un** (*thirty and one*) etc., but for 22, 23, 24, 25, etc., one replaces **et** with a hyphen: **vingt-deux, vingt-trois, vingt-quatre**.

 Practice

1 Match the questions in the left-hand column with the answers on the right.

a C'est_ouvert?

b C'est loin?

c C'est cher?

d C'est combien?

e C'est près?

1 Non, c'est bon marché.

2 Non, c'est_à dix minutes à pied.

3 Oui, c'est tout près.

4 C'est 50€45.

5 Non, c'est fermé.

2 You've just arrived at a hotel. At the reception you find out about the hotel and the amenities in the area. Can you ask the right questions to reconstruct the conversation?

a _____

Non, Monsieur, il n'y a pas de restaurant dans l'hôtel.

b _____

Oui, il y a une pharmacie au bout de la rue.

c _____

Oui, il y a beaucoup de magasins près d'ici.

d _____

Non, Monsieur, la banque est fermée maintenant.

e _____

Oui, il y a un train direct pour Paris.

f _____

Non, la gare n'est pas loin. Elle est_à cinq minutes à pied.

3 That night you have a nightmare; you are in town doing some shopping but it is a very strange town. Using the example as a model, describe what you see to your friend.

Example: Il y a des cartes postales mais_il n'y a pas de timbres.

a _____ une pharmacie _____ aspirine.

b _____ pâtisserie _____ croissants.

c _____ une gare _____ trains.

d _____ un arrêt d'autobus _____ bus.

e _____ un bar _____ bière.

f _____ une cabine téléphonique _____ téléphone.

4 **You overhear one side of a woman's conversation in a café. These are the answers, but what were the questions?**

 a Oui, je suis_en vacances.

 b Oui, je suis mariée.

 c Non, je n'ai pas d'enfants.

 d Non, je n'habite pas Londres, j'habite Manchester.

 e Je travaille comme secrétaire.

5 **Complete the questions using one of the following words: où, quand, quoi, combien.**

 a C'est _____ le journal? C'est 2€11.

 b C'est _____ l'arrêt d'autobus? C'est_au bout de la rue.

 c C'est _____ les vacances? C'est_en juin.

 d C'est _____ la Pyramide? C'est près du Louvre.

 e C'est _____ le Centre Pompidou? C'est_un musée d'art contemporain.

6 04.04 **Listen to how much each item costs and note the price tags in euros.**

 a _____

 b _____

 c _____

 d _____

 e _____

7 04.05 **Listen to the numbers and practise saying them out loud.**
 41 – 42 – 68 – 15 – 5 – 55 – 14 – 29 – 31 – 47 – 60 – 11

8 **Complete the sentences with the correct word from the box.**

 ton sa leurs votre nos ma

 a Il est en vacances avec _____ famille.

 b Elles sont en vacances avec _____ parents.

 c C'est quoi, _____ travail? (formal)

 d C'est quoi, _____ travail? (informal)

 e _____ femme et moi, nous avons trois enfants.

 f _____ enfants ont douze, neuf et deux ans.

9 Sandrine recognizes a man at her bus stop; she strikes up a conversation with him. Put the dialogue in order, starting with 1.

___ Oui, depuis une semaine.

_1_ Bonjour, vous vous_appelez comment?

___ Oui, j'habite au bout de la rue. Vous êtes en vacances ici?

___ Je m'appelle Sandrine. Vous_habitez Paris?

___ Moi, c'est Philippe, et vous?

10 Change the expressions to ones of the same meaning, using **son, sa, ses**. For example, instead of **le magasin de Catherine,** say **son magasin.**

a le travail de Mme Durand

b les amies de Jeanne

c les vacances de Mr Hulot

d la banlieue de Karim

e le parc de Chatou

f la voiture de Mathilde

11 Change the meaning of these sentences by giving the opposite of the highlighted words. Then say the new sentences out loud.

a C'est une petite station de métro.

b Le billet de train pour Paris est bon marché.

c Les magasins sont ouverts le dimanche.

d La pharmacie est près du parc.

Listening and speaking

1 04.06 **Listen as a French tourist asks for help finding her way around an English town. Then make a note of the missing words in the dialogue, and answer the questions.**

Tourist	Pardon, euh … vous parlez _____?
Englishman	Seulement un _____ peu.
Tourist	Je cherche une pharmacie. C'est loin _____?
Englishman	Parlez plus _____, s'il vous plaît.
Tourist	Il y a une pharmacie près d'ici?
Englishman	Oui, Boots est à_dix minutes _____

a What is the communication problem at first?
b What is the French lady looking for?
c Is it near or far?

2 **Now imagine that you are taking part in the conversation with the tourist. Answer the next round of questions according to the prompts.**

You	*Ask the woman if she's on holiday.*
Tourist	Oui, je suis_en vacances avec mon fils depuis une semaine. Nous cherchons une piscine. Il y a une piscine dans cette ville?
You	*Say yes, but it's closed.*
Tourist	Quel dommage! Et il y a peut-être un cinéma?
You	*Say yes. It's far away but the bus stop is at the end of the street.*
Tourist	C'est quel numéro pour l'autobus?
You	*Say it's the 27 bus.*

? Test yourself

1 How would you ask someone in French in a formal way...

a his/her name.

_____

b where he/she lives.

_____

c whether he/she has any children.

_____

d if there is a bank nearby.

_____

e where the bus stop is.

_____

2 How would you tell someone that...

a you don't have any children.

_____

b you live in the suburbs of Paris.

_____

c there are lots of shops nearby.

_____

d the railway station is five minutes away.

_____

e your children work in Paris.

_____

3 Complete the missing numbers in the series. How would you write them out in French?

a 3 – 6 – _____ – 12 – 15 – 18 – _____ – 24 – _____

b 2 – 4 – _____ – 16 – 32 – _____

c _____ – 20 – 30 – _____ – 50 – _____ – 70

SELF CHECK

	I CAN. . .
○	. . . count from 20 to 70.
○	. . . ask simple and useful questions.
○	. . . say that things are mine or somebody else's.
○	. . . understand prices.

5 Quelle heure est-il?
What time is it?

In this unit you will learn:
- ▶ *the days of the week.*
- ▶ *the months of the year.*
- ▶ *some useful expressions of time.*
- ▶ *numbers from 70 to 90.*
- ▶ *dates.*
- ▶ *how to tell the time.*

CEFR: (A1) *Can indicate time by such phrases as next week, last Friday, in November, 3.00, can understand and exchange information about dates, can describe habits and routines.*

French attitude to time

The French tend to have one attitude toward time when they are at work or with strangers and another when they are among friends and family.

When dealing with people you don't know very well, **c'est important d'être ponctuel** (*it's important to be punctual*). Business appointments are always taken on time as a sign of respect. Formal dinner invitations are also punctual affairs and **être en retard** (*to be late*) is seen as a lack of manners.

Customs are much more relaxed among friends and families. It is common to be invited for dinner **vers huit heures** (*around 8 p.m.*) rather than **à huit heures** (*at 8 p.m.*), and **l'apéritif** (*before dinner drinks*) usually stretches long enough to give stragglers time to arrive.

Generally, it's best to be on time, for as the old French saying goes: **Avant l'heure ce n'est pas l'heure, et après l'heure, ce n'est plus l'heure!** (*If you're early, you're not on time, and if you're late, you've missed the time!*)

Do you have to arrive at 20.30 sharp if your French host invites you à huit heures et demie (at 20.30)?

Vocabulary builder

05.01 **Listen and repeat, trying to imitate the native speakers' pronunciation.**

L'HORAIRE *THE TIMETABLE*

À quelle heure...	*At what time...*
*Quand est-ce que l'avion part?	*When does the aircraft leave?*
*Quand est-ce que le bus arrive?	*When does the bus arrive?*
*Quand est-ce qu'on rentre?	*When do we come back?*
*Quand est-ce qu'on peut prendre le petit déjeuner?	*When can we have breakfast?*
*Quand est-ce qu'il y a un métro?	*When is there a (tube, subway) train?*
*Quand finit le concert?	*When does the concert finish?*
Quelle heure est-il?	*What time is it?*
Il est...	*It's...*
dans dix minutes	*in ten minutes' time*
à dix heures du soir	*at ten o'clock in the evening*

LA ROUTINE QUOTIDIENNE *THE DAILY ROUTINE*

tous les jours de la semaine	*every day of the week*
sauf le samedi et le dimanche	*except Saturdays and Sundays*
le lundi, le mardi	*on Mondays, Tuesdays*
et le mercredi	*and Wednesdays*
le jeudi et le vendredi	*on Thursdays and Fridays*
jusqu'à midi/minuit	*until noon/midnight*
depuis dix heures du matin	*since ten in the morning*
pendant l'après-midi	*during the afternoon*
aujourd'hui	*today*
demain	*tomorrow*
maintenant	*now*

NEW EXPRESSIONS

Qu'est-ce que vous faites dans la vie?	*What's your job? (lit. what do you do in life?)*
Je travaille...	*I work...*
Je regarde la télévision.	*I watch TV.*

Remember that you can make the same questions easier by placing the question word afterwards:

L'avion part quand?	*When does the plane leave?*
Le bus arrive quand?	*When does the bus arrive?*

Can you work out a simpler way of asking the questions marked with an asterisk in l'horaire?

Conversation

05.02 *Jane asks Mme Durand about her working week.*
Play the audio several times, and then answer the questions.
a Where does Mme Durand go for lunch?

Jane	Mme Durand, qu'est-ce-que vous faites dans la vie?
Mme Durand	Je suis professeure de biologie.
Jane	Vous travaillez tous les jours?
Mme Durand	Oui, je travaille à temps plein, donc tous les jours sauf le dimanche.
Jane	À quelle heure est-ce que vous commencez le matin?
Mme Durand	Ça dépend, le lundi, le mercredi et le vendredi, je commence à huit heures et demie, mais le mardi et le jeudi je ne travaille pas le matin.
Jane	À quelle heure finissez-vous l'après-midi?
Mme Durand	Je finis à cinq heures et demie le lundi, le mardi, le jeudi et le vendredi. Le mercredi après-midi je ne travaille pas mais je reste dans mon bureau. Le samedi, l'école finit à midi et c'est le week-end jusqu'au lundi matin.
Jane	Où est-ce que vous déjeunez à midi?
Mme Durand	Mes_enfants et moi, nous déjeunons_à l'école. Il y a une cafétéria qui est_ouverte toute la journée de neuf heures à cinq heures.
Jane	Et le week-end, qu'est-ce que vous faites?
Mme Durand	Ah, le week-end c'est formidable mais_il passe trop vite.

donc	*therefore*	qui est_ouverte	*which is open*
ça dépend	*it depends*	formidable	*great*
mais je reste	*but I stay*	il passe trop vite	*it goes too quickly*
le bureau	*the office*		

b Which mornings does Mrs Durand have off?

c How long is her weekend?

LES MOIS DE L'ANNÉE *THE MONTHS OF THE YEAR*

 05.03 **Look at the months of the year. Complete the missing English words, then listen to the French pronunciation.**

janvier	*January*	**juillet**	*July*
février	*February*	**août**	*August*
mars	_____	**septembre**	_____
avril	_____	**octobre**	_____
mai	_____	**novembre**	_____
juin	*June*	**décembre**	*December*

NUMBERS 70–90

05.04 **Work out the missing French numbers. Then listen to the way the French pronounce them.**

_____	70	**quatre-vingts**	80
soixante et onze	71	**quatre-vingt-un**	81
soixante-douze	72	**quatre-vingt-deux**	82
soixante-treize	73	**quatre-vingt-trois**	83
soixante-quatorze	74	**quatre-vingt-quatre**	84
soixante-quinze	75	**quatre-vingt-cinq**	85
soixante-seize	76	_____	86
soixante-dix-sept	77	_____	87
_____	78	**quatre-vingt-huit**	88
soixante-dix-neuf	79	**quatre-vingt-neuf**	89
		quatre-vingt-dix	90

What do you notice about the way 80 is spelt, compared to 81, 82, etc?

> The French sometimes have a tendency to complicate things! Ninety in French is *four twenty ten*. In the next unit you will learn that for 99 you need to say *four twenty ten nine*!

Language discovery

1 THREE DIFFERENT WAYS TO ASK A QUESTION

a By giving a questioning tone to what is really a statement:

Tu es française?   *Are you French?*

b By leaving the verb as it is and using **est-ce que** (pronounced 'esker') which is the equivalent of the English ***do/does***, in sentences such as do you speak English?

Est-ce que tu travailles?   *Do you work?*

Où est-ce que tu habites?   *Where do you live?*

c By turning the verb round and joining the two parts with a hyphen:

Travailles-tu?   *Do you work?*

Out of the three different ways of asking a question, **b** is most commonly heard as there are no situations in which **est-ce que** cannot be used; **a** is common in conversation but less so in written French; **c** is not usually used with **je**.

2 QUESTIONS STARTING WITH *QU'EST-CE QUE...? WHAT...?*

Qu'est-ce que c'est?   *What's that?*

Qu'est-ce que vous désirez?   *What would you like? (in a shop)*

Qu'est-ce que vous faites   *What's your job?*
dans la vie?

Qu'est-ce que can also be replaced by **quoi** and placed at the end:

C'est **quoi?**   *What's that?*

Vous désirez **quoi?**   *What would you like?*

Vous faites **quoi** dans la vie?   *What's your job?*

> Questions with **est-ce que** (think of it as *do* or *does*) call for 'yes' or 'no' answers. When you start the question with **qu'est-ce que** (*what*) expect a wide range of replies.

3 VERBS ENDING IN -IR AND -RE

There are three main groups of regular verbs in French:

▶ verbs ending in **-er** e.g. **travailler**
▶ verbs ending in **-ir** e.g. **finir**
▶ verbs ending in **-re** e.g. **attendre**

To work out the present tense of **-ir** and **-re** verbs, knock the **-ir** and **-re** off the infinitives and then add the following endings:

finir (to finish)		attendre (to wait)	
je	fin**is**	j'	att**ends**
tu	fin**is**	tu	attend**s**
il/elle/on	fin**it**	il/elle/on	attend
nous	fin**issons**	nous	attend**ons**
vous	fin**issez**	vous	attend**ez**
ils/elles	fin**issent**	ils/elles	attend**ent**

À quelle heure **finissez-vous?** — *At what time do you finish?*

Je finis à 5h.30. — *I finish at 5.30.*

L'école finit à midi. — *School finishes at lunchtime.*

J'attends le train de 7h.30. — *I'm waiting for the 7.30 train.*

Elle attend son petit_ami. — *She's waiting for her boyfriend.*

Remember not to pronounce the last letters in: finis/finit/finissons/finiss**ent**; attends/attend/attendons/attend**ent**.

4 GIVING THE DATE

The English talk about the 1st, 2nd, 3rd, 4th, etc. ... of the month. The French say 'the 1st' (**le premier** or **1er**) but 'the two', 'the three', 'the four', etc. ... of the month:

Quelle est la date? — *What's the date?*

Nous sommes **le 1er_octobre**. — *It's the 1st October.*

Aujourd'hui c'est **le deux_avril**. — *Today is the 2nd of April.*

5 TELLING THE TIME

The 24-hour clock is used widely in France to distinguish between a.m. and p.m.

il est treize heures — *it's 1 p.m.*

il est quatorze heures quinze — *it's 2.15 p.m.*

il est quinze heures trente — *it's 3.30 p.m.*

il est seize heures quarante-cinq   *it's 4.45 p.m.*

il est dix-sept heures cinquante   *it's 5.50 p.m.*

To reply to the question **Quelle heure est-il?** *What time is it?*, it is more common to use the 12-hour clock:

- **a** il est dix heures
- **b** il est dix heures cinq
- **c** il est dix heures et quart (lit. *ten hours and a quarter*)
- **d** il est dix heures et demie (lit. *ten hours and half*)

- **e** il est onze heures moins vingt-cinq (lit. *eleven hours minus twenty-five*)
- **f** il est onze heures moins vingt
- **g** il est onze heures moins le quart (lit. *eleven hours minus the quarter*)
- **h** il est onze heures moins dix
- **i** il est onze heures moins cinq

To distinguish between 9 a.m. and 9 p.m. people say:

il est neuf heures du matin   *it's 9 a.m.*

il est neuf heures du soir   *it's 9 p.m.*

> Pronounce the **f** of **neuf** as a **v** when it is followed by a vowel or an **h**.

Noon and midnight are however distinguished from each other:

il est midi   *it's (12 p.m.) midday*

il est minuit   *it's (12 a.m.) midnight*

6 FAIRE *TO DO/TO MAKE*

Faire is an irregular verb as it does not follow the pattern of **attendre**. It is used in a number of expressions in French (can you think of a recent one you've seen?). Here is a new one: **faire la cuisine** *to do the cooking*:

je fais	**nous faisons**
tu fais	**vous faites**
il/elle/on fait	**ils/elles font**

7 PRENDRE *TO TAKE*

Prendre is also an irregular verb and needs to be learnt on its own. **Apprendre** *to learn* and **comprendre** *to understand* follow the same pattern as **prendre**:

je prends	**nous prenons**
tu prends	**vous prenez**
Il/elle/on prend	**ils/elles prennent**

Practice

1 **Complete the sentences with the correct form of the verbs in brackets.**

a Le matin je _____ (prendre) le train à 7.30.

b Mes_enfants _____ (commencer) l'école à 8.30.

c Le train _____ (arriver) à huit heures du matin.

d Il _____ (apprendre) le français depuis deux mois.

e À midi on _____ (déjeuner) à la cafétéria.

f Qu'est-ce que vous _____ (prendre) pour le petit déjeuner?

g De huit heures à neuf_heures je _____ (faire) la cuisine.

h Quelle heure _____ (être)-il?

i Le mercredi, la journée _____ (finir) à midi.

j Qu'est-ce que vous _____ (faire) dans la vie?

k Nous _____ (attendre) à l'arrêt d'autobus.

l Ils _____ (comprendre) l'anglais.

2 Complete the questions by selecting the appropriate endings.

a	Comment	**1**	vous faites dans la vie?
b	Quel âge	**2**	une banque près d'ici?
c	C'est où	**3**	vous_appelez-vous?
d	Qu'est-ce que	**4**	commencez-vous le matin?
e	Il y a	**5**	la cabine téléphonique?
f	À quelle heure	**6**	combien d'enfants?
g	Vous_avez	**7**	ont-ils?

3 Below is M. Durand's timetable for a typical day. However, the lines got muddled up. Can you put them in the right order, starting with 1.

jusqu'à	until
de ... à...	from ... to...
avec	with
vers	around

_____	**a**	Il arrive au travail à 9 heures.
_____	**b**	Le soir, il regarde la télévision jusqu'à 22 heures.
_____	**c**	Il travaille de 9.15 à 13 heures.
_____	**d**	Il finit la journée à 17.30.
_____	**e**	Il prend le train à 7 heures du matin.
__1__	**f**	Il prend le petit déjeuner à 6.30 du matin.
_____	**g**	À midi il déjeune au restaurant avec ses collègues.
_____	**h**	Il rentre à la maison vers 19.15.

4 Give the following dates in French:

a 1st May

b 3rd February

c 21st March

d 15th July

e 10th June

f 13th October

g 30th September

h 6th August

5 Using the pictures to help you, fill in the missing words.

a

b

c

d

e

f

g

h

a Je _____ le petit déjeuner.
b Ils _____ le train.
c Elle _____ le travail à 9h.
d Il _____ jusqu'à midi.
e À midi il _____ à la cafétéria.
f Le soir il _____ le travail à 17.30.
g Elle _____ la cuisine.
h Ils _____ la télévision.

6 05.05 **Listen to Michel talking about what he's going to do this week. Note the day (in French) next to each activity Michel has planned. (aller = *to go*).**

a _____ je déjeune au restaurant avec Sophie.

b _____ je prends le train pour Manchester.

c _____ je regarde la télévision avec ma famille.

d _____ j'achète des fleurs pour ma femme.

7 **You're being asked to take part in a survey at the railway station. Give the answers according to the prompts.**

Question A quelle heure prenez-vous le train?

You _____ (à 7.20)

Question Et vous commencez le travail à quelle heure?

You _____ (à 9h du matin)

Question Qu'est-ce que vous faites dans le train?

You _____ (prendre un café)

Question Vous lisez le journal?

You _____ (non/écouter un podcast)

8 **What time is it? Answer using the 12-hour clock. To differentiate between a.m. and p.m. you can use du matin/de l'après midi/du soir. Use also midi and minuit to distinguish between the middle of the day and the middle of the night.**

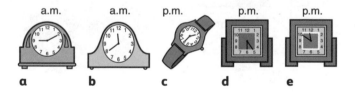

a.m.   a.m.   p.m.   p.m.   p.m.

a   b   c   d   e

? Test yourself

1 **Can you answer these questions in French?**

   a What are the five days of the working week?

   _____

   b Which are the first three months of the year?

   _____

   c What is the date of New Year's Day?

   _____

2 **Complete the sentences with the correct form of the verb.**

   a Nous _____ (comprendre) l'italien.

   b Le samedi, l'école _____ (finir) à midi.

   c Vous _____ (regarder) la télévision le soir ?

   d Qu'est-ce que vous _____ (faire) dans la vie ?

3 **Which two sentences mean the same thing?**

   a Il est onze heures moins le quart.

   b Il est vingt-deux heures quarante-cinq.

   c Il est midi moins le quart.

SELF CHECK

	I CAN. . .
○	. . . count up to 90.
●	. . . name the days of the week and the months of the year.
●	. . . tell the date and the time.

6

Pour aller à…?
The way to…?

In this unit you will learn:
▶ *how to count from 90 upwards.*
▶ *how to ask for and understand directions.*

CEFR: (A1) *Can ask for and give specific directions referring to a map or a plan, can understand relevant information and ask for repetition of key points.*

Asking your way

Even with **un plan de la ville** (*a town map*), if you're visiting new places in France it is inevitable that, **tôt ou tard** (*sooner or later*), you will need to ask for directions. Local people all have their **points de repère** (*landmarks*), which can be **les grands magasins** (*department stores*) in large cities, or **la place** (*the town square*) in a village.

Understanding the directions people give you can be a little challenging. It helps to focus on key verbs like **il faut passer…** (*you have to go beyond…*) or **continuez** (*carry on*). You must also pay attention to people's body language for cues such as **tournez à gauche** (*turn left*) or **c'est tout droit** (*it's straight ahead*). The French are likely to point the way with their hands and arms. And if you're still unsure, don't hesitate to throw up your hands and say **'Encore une fois? Je ne suis pas d'ici!'** (*One more time? I'm not from here.*)

What French word is used to mark the difference between a store and a department store?
What French expression might you use to ask someone to repeat what they have just said?

Vocabulary builder

06.01 **Read along as you listen to the new expressions. Then, hide the English translations and try to remember the meanings.**

(VOUS) ALLEZ TOUT DROIT *(YOU) GO STRAIGHT ON*

pour_aller à…	*the way to…*
continuez	*carry on*
descendez la rue	*go down the street*
montez l'avenue	*go up the avenue*
passez le magasin	*go beyond the shop*
traversez la place	*cross the square*
prenez la route de…	*take the road to…*

VOUS TOURNEZ… *YOU TURN…*

tournez à gauche	*turn left*
tournez à droite	*turn right*
vous_allez prendre …	*you're going to take …*
la première rue à droite	*the first street on the right*
la deuxième sur votre gauche	*the second on your left*

OÙ EST LE PARC? *WHERE IS THE PARK?*

la place du marché est située…	*the market place is…*
au coin de la rue	*at the corner of the street*
à côté du supermarché	*next to the supermarket*
en face de la boulangerie	*opposite the baker's*
au centre ville	*in the town centre*
sur votre gauche	*on your left*
sur, sous	*on, under*
devant, derrière	*in front of, behind*
dans	*in, inside*
entre	*between*
il faut combien de temps ?	*how long does it take?*
il faut environ 25 minutes	*it takes about 25 minutes*

What are the French words for *left* and *right*?

Now match the words and their meaning.

a	en face de…	**1**	at the corner
b	au coin	**2**	next (to)
c	derrière	**3**	in front of…
d	à côté	**4**	behind

Conversation

Jane is spending the day with the Durands. She decides to go to the town centre in the afternoon.

 1 06.02 **Listen as you look at the street map (le plan de la ville) of Chatou in this unit. Then try answering the question.**

How do you get from M. Durand's house to the park and how long does it take to walk there?

Jane	M. Durand, avez-vous un plan de Chatou? Je voudrais_aller d'abord au parc et puis, si j'ai le temps, dans les magasins …
M. Durand	Voici le plan. Vous pouvez le garder car j'en_ai deux.
Jane	Merci beaucoup. Où est le parc de Chatou?
M. Durand	Voyons, nous sommes_ici sur le plan. Vous tournez à gauche en sortant de la maison, vous_allez jusqu'au bout de la rue Vaugirard, vous tournez à droite dans la rue Vincennes et puis c'est sur votre gauche à 200 mètres.
Jane	Bon, alors, à gauche en sortant puis je tourne à droite et c'est sur ma gauche … C'est loin à pied?
M. Durand	Non, pas très loin; il faut environ 25 minutes.
Jane	Oh là là, c'est trop loin pour moi. Euh, on peut y aller en_autobus?
M. Durand	Oui, oui. L'arrêt d'autobus est situé juste au coin de la rue Vaugirard. C'est très pratique et il y a un autobus toutes les dix minutes.
Jane	Je voudrais aussi faire des_achats pour moi et acheter quelques souvenirs pour ma famille en Grande-Bretagne et au Canada.
M. Durand	Eh bien, vous pouvez_aller au centre commercial. Il est sur la place du marché à côté de la gare. Vous_avez un_autobus direct. Il va du parc au centre commercial.
Jane	Bon, je pars tout de suite … j'ai beaucoup de choses à acheter et … je voudrais rentrer vers 19 heures.

Language discovery

d'abord	firstly
si j'ai le temps	if I have the time
voici	here is
le garder	keep it
voyons	let's see
en sortant de	as you leave
la maison	the house
trop loin	too far
faire des_achats	to do some shopping
le centre commercial	the shopping centre
je pars	I leave

1 ASKING THE WAY AND GIVING DIRECTIONS

Pour aller à (*to get to*) is a very useful structure to remember. Used in a questioning tone it means *How do I/we get to…?*

Pardon, Monsieur, pour aller à Gordes?	*Excuse me, Sir, how do we get to Gordes?*
Pour aller à Gordes, prenez la route pour St. Saturnin.	*To get to Gordes, take the road to St Saturnin.*

2 ALLER TO GO

Aller is an irregular verb. It is particularly useful as it is used when speaking about the future (explained in Unit 10):

je vais

tu vas

il/elle/on va

nous allons

vous allez

ils/elles vont

Vous_**allez** jusqu'au bout de la rue.
You go to the end of the road.

Je voudrais aller à la banque.
I would like to go to the bank.

3 UNDERSTANDING DIRECTIONS

Understanding directions can be trickier than asking the way as the directions can sound complicated, so it is important to pick out the essential words and repeat them out loud as they are given to you:

a   As an answer to your question, you'll probably hear one of the following constructions:

Il faut prendre…	*You have to (lit. it's necessary to) take…*
Il faut descendre…	*You have to go down…*
Il faut tourner…	*You have to turn…*

Il faut aller...	You have to go...
Il faut monter...	You have to go up...

b The **t** in **droite** *right* is sounded but it is not in **droit** *straight*. **Droit** is usually preceded by **tout: tout droit** *straight on*. **Droite** is preceded by **à** or **sur la: à drojte, sur la droite:**

Il faut aller **tout droit**.	You have to go straight on.
La gare est **sur la droite**.	The station is on the right.

c You may be unlucky when asking directions and find that you are asking a tourist! His answer would be **je ne sais pas** (*I don't know*), or **je ne suis pas d'ici** (*I am not from here*).

4 WHEN TO USE *À*; WHEN TO USE *EN*

To say that you are in town or you are going/want to go to a town, always use **à** (with an accent to differentiate it from **a** *has*). Study the examples below:

Je suis à Bordeaux.	*I'm in Bordeaux.*
Nous_allons à Bordeaux.	*We're going to Bordeaux.*

To say that you are in a country or you're going to a country, use **en** with feminine countries (often finishing with an **-e**) and **au/aux** with the others:

Je suis en_Australie.	*I am in Australia.*
Je vais en_Angleterre.	*I'm going to England.*
Vous_allez au Canada.	*You're going to Canada.*

The country is preceded by its article in sentences such as:

Je connais bien la Suisse.	*I know Switzerland quite well.*
J'aime beaucoup le Portugal.	*I like Portugal a lot.*

5 WHEN *À* (AT, TO, IN, ON) IS FOLLOWED BY *LE, LA, L', LES*

The preposition **à** followed by a definite article (**le**, **la**, **l'**, **les**) changes its form in the following way:

à + le	becomes	au
à + la	remains	à la
à + l'	remains	à l'
à + les	becomes	aux

> It's easy! Use **à** before towns and **en** before countries, or **au** with the few masculine ones.

Pour aller **au musée** du Louvre, s'il vous plaît?	*Which way to the Louvre Museum please?*
Nous_allons **à l'église** St. Paul.	*We are going to St Paul's Church.*
Il arrive **à la gare** à huit heures du matin.	*He arrives at the station at eight o'clock in the morning.*
Il va **aux_États-Unis** deux fois par mois.	*He goes to the United States twice a month.*

💡 **How would you complete these sentences? Je voudrais aller _____ cinéma. Vous allez _____ parc? Elles vont _____ piscine le jeudi. Ma grand-mère va _____ hôpital.**

6 LOCATING THE EXACT SPOT

Remember that when **de** is used in combination with **le, la, l', les** in expressions such as **en face de** *opposite*, **à côté de** *next to*, **au coin de** *at the corner of*, **près de** *near*, you need to change its form (Unit 2):

au coin **du parc**	*at the corner of the park*
près **des grands magasins**	*near the department stores*
en face **de la piscine**	*opposite the swimming pool*
à côté **de l'office du tourisme**	*next to the tourist office*

💡 **Try saying in French:** *It's opposite the department stores. I am on the street corner.*

7 NUMBERS OVER 90

🎧 06.03

quatre-vingt-dix	*90*	**cent**	*100*
quatre-vingt-onze	*91*	**cent un**	*101*
quatre-vingt-douze	*92*	**cent deux**	*102*
quatre-vingt-treize	*93*	**cent vingt-trois**	*123*
quatre-vingt-quatorze	*94*	**cinq cent trente-quatre**	*534*
quatre-vingt-quinze	*95*	**mille**	*1000*
quatre-vingt-seize	*96*	**mille neuf cent quinze**	*1915*
quatre-vingt-dix-sept	*97*	**deux mille**	*2000*
quatre-vingt-dix-huit	*98*		
quatre-vingt-dix-neuf	*99*		

How would you write out 149 and 3,000 in French?

8 PREMIER, DEUXIÈME, TROISIÈME *FIRST, SECOND, THIRD*

If you are directed to the 3rd floor, the 2nd street and so on, the numbers end in **-ième**:

deuxième	*second*	**quatrième**	*fourth*
troisième	*third*	**dixième**	*tenth*

But, *first* is **premier** before all masculine nouns, and **première** before all feminine nouns:

Vous montez au **premier** étage.   *You go up to the first floor.*

C'est la **première** porte.   *It is the first door.*

Vous prenez la **deuxième** à gauche.   *You take the second on the left.*

C'est le **troisième** bâtiment.   *It's the third building.*

How would you tell someone in a lift that you want the fifth floor?

 Practice

1   **You are Jane, visiting Chatou for the first time. How would you ask a passer-by the way to:**

a la piscine

b la gare

c l'église St Paul

d le musée

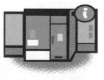

e l'office du tourisme

2 06.04 **Now listen to the replies of the passers-by and work out which letter on the map stands for each of these places.**

a C'est très facile. Vous montez la rue Vincennes et vous prenez la première à gauche. La piscine se trouve sur votre droite, en face du parc.

b Bon, pour la gare, continuez tout droit, toujours tout droit. Juste avant le pont, tournez à droite et vous_êtes dans la rue Thiers. La gare est_à côté du centre commercial.

c L'église St Paul? Eh bien, c'est tout droit, à 100 mètres d'ici, sur votre droite, au coin de la rue Fleurus.

d Euh – attendez voir – il faut tourner tout de suite à droite puis descendez la rue Fleurus et le musée est_à 10 minutes à pied sur votre gauche à côté de l'Hôtel Colbert.

e Vous_allez tout droit jusqu'au pont. Juste avant le pont tournez à gauche et l'office du tourisme se trouve à côté d'une pharmacie.

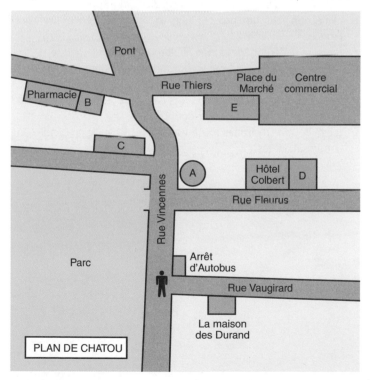

3 Now it's your turn to practise giving directions. Imagine you are standing **au coin de la rue Vaugirard et de la rue de Vincennes à Chatou.** Look at the **plan de Chatou** and answer the questions.

a Pour aller à la pharmacie, s'il vous plaît?

b Je voudrais aller à l'hôtel Colbert; pouvez-vous me dire où il se trouve?

c Savez-vous où est le centre commercial?

d Je ne suis pas d'ici ... euh, c'est loin la rue Thiers?

Use Exercise 2 as a model, but vary your answers. For example instead of **vous montez/descendez la rue** you can say **(vous) allez/continuez tout droit.** (The answers are not given in the Answer key.)

06.05 **Essayez!** *Have a go!* Now listen to some ways of responding.

4 Choose the right expression to complete the sentences. Then practise saying them out loud.

a Jane habite à Brighton?/en Brighton?/de Brighton?

b Elle et son petit_ami passent leurs vacances en France/au France/France.

c mais_ils préfèrent Allemagne./l'Allemagne./en Allemagne.

d Cet_été (*this summer*) elle va au Danemark/Danemark/en Danemark où elle a des_amis.

e Son petit_ami va souvent en États-Unis/aux_États-Unis/les_États-Unis et au Japon./en Japon./Japon.

f Il est_homme d'affaires (*businessman*) et travaille en Londres./à Londres./Londres.

5 Look at the **centre commercial de Chatou** and complete the sentences using the words from the list.

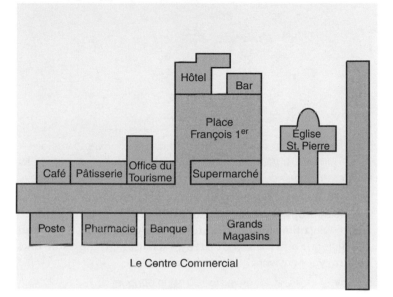

à côté de la   en face du   dans la rue   entre   grands magasins
pâtisserie   sur la place   au coin de   au bout de   bar

a La poste est _____ café.
b Le café est _____ pâtisserie.
c L'office du tourisme est _____ la place François 1er.
d La pharmacie est _____ la poste et la banque.
e L'église est _____ la rue Thiers.
f Les _____ sont en face du supermarché.
g Le _____ est à côté de l'hôtel.
h La _____ est entre le café et l'office du tourisme.
i La pharmacie est _____ Thiers.
j Le supermarché est _____ François 1er.

6 Test your knowledge of numbers. Pick numbers from the box below and say them out loud in French.

72	24	80	92	65
	43	75	61	
76	68		15	66
17	96		87	70
19	21	49	55	65
	56	13	77	

Repeat the exercise over a number of days and see if you can improve your performance. If you find it difficult, go back to Units 3–5 and review the French numbers you have learnt so far.

7 06.06 **You are in the shopping centre in Chatou. A French passer-by stops you and asks about the shops. To take part in the conversation, look at the street map in Exercise 5. First read the dialogue and plan what to say, then listen to the audio and confirm your answers.**

Passer-by	Je ne suis pas d'ici. Où est la banque?
You	*The bank is next to the chemist's.*
Passer-by	Merci beaucoup. Je voudrais acheter quelques souvenirs pour ma famille. Où sont les grands magasins?
You	*They are opposite the supermarket.*
Passer-by	Il faut combien de temps pour aller au supermarché?
You	*It takes about 15 minutes on foot.*
Passer-by	Merci. Et ... où est la poste?
You	*It's opposite the café.*
Passer-by	Elle est_ouverte maintenant?
You	*No, it's shut but it opens at 2 o'clock.*
Passer-by	Ah merci beaucoup.

? Test yourself

1 Match the words and their meanings.

a la boulangerie   **1** the swimming pool

b le centre commercial   **2** the bakery

c le grand magasin   **3** on the second floor

d la piscine   **4** a shopping centre

e au deuxième étage   **5** a department store

2 Complete the missing numbers in each series. How would you write them out?

a   91 ————   95   97 ————   101

b   125 ————   115   110 ————   100

c   ————   80   90   100 ————   120

d   ————   1250   1350 ————   1550

3 Pair the words with their opposites.

a devant   **1** à droite

b à gauche   **2** descendez

c sur   **3** derrière

d montez   **4** sous

e allez tout droit   **5** tournez

SELF CHECK

I CAN...
○   ... count and use numbers from 90 upwards.
○   ... ask for and understand directions.

7 C'est comment?
What is it like?

In this unit you will learn how to:
▶ *name colours.*
▶ *describe things and people.*
▶ *say precisely what you want.*
▶ *compare people and objects.*

CEFR: (A1) *Can ask about things and make simple transactions in shops, Can make simple purchases by stating what is wanted and asking the price, Can use simple descriptive language to compare objects and people.*

The meaning of colours

In France as in the rest of the western world, **les couleurs** (*colours*) have meaning. They **représentent** (*represent, stand for*) human emotions and qualities, or things found in **la nature** (*the natural world*). Knowing **le sens des couleurs** (*the meaning of colours*) can help you remember their names better.

Test your intuition and match the colours below with the words they best represent. You can take a reasonable guess at understanding the French words you don't know: they're similar to their English equivalents.

a	**blanc**	*white*	1	la passion et le danger
b	**bleu**	*blue*	2	la nature et la stabilité
c	**marron**	*brown*	3	le café et la neutralité
d	**orange**	*orange*	4	l'océan, la loyauté
e	**rouge**	*red*	5	la pureté et l'innocence
f	**jaune**	*yellow*	6	la sécurité et l'optimisme
g	**noir**	*black*	7	la fête et la joie
h	**vert**	*green*	8	l'élégance et la rigueur

07.01 Play the audio or look at the bottom of the page to see how well you did. Then hide the colour names and try to remember them by looking only at their meanings.

a 5, b 4, c 3, d 6, e 1, f 7, g 8, h 2

🎙 Vocabulary builder

07.02 **Listen to the new vocabulary, then repeat and try to imitate the pronunciation of the speakers.**

FAIRE DES_ACHATS *TO DO SOME SHOPPING*

faire des courses	*to run errands*
dépenser	*to spend*
qu'est-ce que vous_avez comme...	*what do you have in the way of...*
souvenirs/cadeaux?	*souvenirs/presents*
vous_avez autre chose?	*do you have anything else?*
ça coûte combien?	*how much is it?*
c'est de quelle couleur?	*what colour is it?*
je cherche quelque chose...	*I'm looking for something...*
pour comparer	*to compare*
grand/moyen/petit	*big/medium/small*
un peu plus grand	*a little bigger*
un peu moins cher	*a little less expensive*
meilleur marché	*cheaper*
spécial/différent	*special/different*
je vais prendre le plus petit	*I'll take the smallest*

KEY EXPRESSIONS

il porte des lunettes de soleil	*he wears/is wearing sunglasses*
elle porte une chemise unie	*she wears/is wearing a plain shirt*
il a les cheveux noirs et raides	*he has black, straight hair*
elle a les yeux marron/bruns	*she has brown eyes*

💡 **What expression does French use to mean** *a little*?

Conversation

Jane is shopping in a department store in Chatou. She is looking for something special to take back to her mother in the UK.

07.03 Listen to the dialogue, then answer the questions.

a What is Jane looking for?

Vendeuse	Vous désirez?
Jane	Je cherche un souvenir pour ma mère ... euh quelque chose de spécial pour ramener en Angleterre.
Vendeuse	Bon, très bien. Alors si c'est pour votre mère, je peux vous montrer des foulards en soie avec des scènes typiquement françaises.
Jane	Oh, ils sont très jolis et leurs couleurs sont vraiment superbes. C'est combien?
Vendeuse	Alors, les grands coûtent 68€50 et 53€ et les petits 46€.
Jane	Je peux voir ceux qui sont à 46€?
Vendeuse	Mais bien sûr. Ils représentent les monuments célèbres de Paris. Certains sont rouges et bleus, d'autres verts et jaunes.
Jane	Je préfère les grands, mais_ils sont trop chers et je ne veux pas trop dépenser.
Vendeuse	Alors, il vaut mieux prendre un petit à 46€.
Jane	Oui, je vais prendre ce petit qui représente l'Arc de Triomphe. Ses couleurs bleues et rouges sont superbes et il n'est pas trop cher. Je crois que ma mère sera très contente.

> **ramener** *to bring back*
> **je peux vous montrer** *I can show you*
> **foulard (m) en soie** *a silk scarf*
> **joli(e)** *pretty*
> **ceux qui...** *the ones which...*
> **célèbres** *famous*
> **certains ... d'autres** *some ... others*
> **il vaut mieux prendre** *you should take (lit. it is better to take)*
> **je crois que** *I believe that*
> **sera contente** *will be pleased*

b Why does Jane buy the small scarf?

c What colour scarf does she choose eventually?

Language discovery

1 CE, CET, CETTE, CES *THIS, THAT, THESE, THOSE*

Ce, **cet**, **cette** all mean *this* or *that*; **ces** means *these* or *those*. **Ce** comes before masculine singular nouns, **cet** before masculine singular nouns beginning with a vowel or silent **h**, **cette** before feminine singular nouns and **ces** before plural nouns:

	masculine	masc. (before a vowel or silent h)	feminine
singular	ce	cet	cette
plural	ces	ces	ces

ce foulard	*this/that scarf*
cet_homme	*this/that man*
cette femme	*this/that woman (**femme**, pronounced 'fam', also means 'wife')*
ces_enfants	*these/those children*

> 💡 **Can you work out the plural of ce magasin and cette chose?**

2 SAYING PRECISELY WHAT YOU WANT

You already know how to ask for something, e.g. **je voudrais cette bouteille**. This is the most general way of asking for things, but you may want to give more information.

a How much? Expressions of quantity are linked with **de**:

Combien **d'**enfants?	*How many children?*
beaucoup **d'**enfants	*lots of children*
un verre **de** vin	*a glass of wine*
une boîte **de** haricots	*a tin of beans*

> 💡 **How would you say: *I have many friends*?**

b Made of what? You can use **de** or **en** to say what things are made of:

une chemise **de** coton	*a cotton shirt*
une robe **en** soie	*a silk dress*

c **What kind?** Add adjectives to describe in more detail:

un verre de vin **rouge**	*a glass of red wine*
une boîte de **petits** pois français	*a tin of French peas*
un kilo de raisins **noirs**	*a kilo of black grapes*

d **What's in/on it?** Special features such as patterns, flavours or key ingredients are linked with **à**:

un yaourt **à** l'abricot	*an apricot yoghurt*
un sandwich **au** fromage	*a cheese sandwich*
une glace **à** la vanille	*a vanilla ice cream*
une tarte **aux** pommes	*an apple pie*

Don't forget to change the **à** to **au** or to **aux** if the following noun is masculine or plural.

e **With/without.** Put **avec** (*with*) or **sans** (*without*) in front of what you want or don't want:

une chambre **avec** télévision	*a room with (a) television*
un hôtel **sans** parking	*a hotel without car park*

3 HOW ADJECTIVES WORK

As explained in Unit 3, adjectives change according to what they are describing; they may take masculine, feminine or plural forms:

	masculine	feminine
singular	petit	petite
plural	petits	petites

ce **petit** foulard	*this little scarf*
c'est_une **bonne** école	*it's a good school*
les **petits** pois sont verts	*peas are green*
avec des scènes **françaises**	*with French scenes*

a Adding an **-e** to the masculine (if it has not already got an **-e**) to form the feminine often changes the pronunciation, as in **petit** (m), **petite** (f), but not always, e.g. **noir** (m), **noire** (f), **bleu** (m), **bleue** (f). The **-s** in the plural is not sounded.

b **Brun** is used almost exclusively to refer to the colour of someone's hair, eyes or complexion. For most brown objects, use **marron**, which is an invariable form.

c A few adjectives have two masculine forms: the second one is used in front of nouns beginning with a vowel or silent **h**:

le **nouveau** garçon	the new boy
le **nouvel_**élève	the new pupil
le **vieux** port	the old harbour
le **vieil_**hôtel	the old hotel

d Adjectives are usually placed after the noun:

un café **noir**	a black coffee
une bière **brune**	brown ale

except with common ones such as: **petit** (*small*), **bon(ne)** (*good*), **beau** (*beautiful*), **grand** (*tall*), **jeune** (*young*), **vieux** (*old*), **mauvais** (*bad*), **joli** (*beautiful*), **tout** (*all*):

un **grand** café	a large coffee
une **bonne** bière	a good beer

e If there are two or more adjectives they are placed after the noun and linked with **et**, or they are placed either side of the noun:

des cheveux **blonds et longs**	long, blond hair
un **grand** homme **mince**	a tall, slim man

4 MAKING COMPARISONS

To say that something is *more ... than* or *less ... than* use:

plus ... que	more ... than
moins ... que	less ... than
Le train est **plus rapide que** la voiture.	The train is faster than the car.
Il est **moins grand que** moi.	He's less tall than I.

5 SAYING 'BETTER'

To say that something/someone is *better*, use **meilleur(e)**; to say that you do something *better* use **mieux**:

Le film est **meilleur** que le livre. *The film is better than the book.*

Elle parle français **mieux** que moi. *She speaks French better than I.*

Whereas there is only one word *better* in English, there are two in French. It is easy to differentiate between them, however. **Meilleur** goes with things, e.g. books, films, food, whereas **mieux** goes with how you do things.

 Practice

1 **Complete the dialogue with ce, cet, cette or ces. To check if the words are masculine or feminine, look at the French–English vocabulary.**

À la gare routière

Touriste Pardon Monsieur, _____ autobus va à Quimper?

Homme Oui, Madame, tous _____ autobus vont à Quimper.

Touriste Je voudrais partir _____ matin. A quelle heure partent les_autobus?

Homme Bon, _____ deux_autobus partent pour Quimper _____ matin. Le premier part à 8.30 et arrive à 12.00 et le deuxième part à 9.15 et arrive à 13.15 _____ après-midi.

Touriste Très bien. Je veux rentrer _____ nuit. À quelle heure rentre le dernier_autobus de Quimper?

Homme Alors _____ semaine, le dernier bus quitte Quimper à 20.30.

2 07.04 **Using M. Durand's description as a model, write a few sentences about what Mme Durand and Jane look like. Make sure that the adjectives agree with the nouns they describe. You can look up words you don't know in the French–English vocabulary.**

	M. Durand	Mme Durand	Jane
sexe	homme	femme	femme
âge	40 ans	35 ans	23 ans
cheveux	noirs/raides	blonds/longs	bruns/courts
yeux	marron	verts	bleus
taille	1,78 mètre	1,70 mètre	1,62 mètre
poids	79 kg	65 kg	55 kg
signes particuliers	moustache	lunettes rondes	–
vêtements	costume bleu marine, cravate jaune, chaussures noires	ensemble vert uni, chemise blanche, chaussures légères	jean bleu pâle, pull-over blanc, bottes noires

Monsieur Durand a 40 ans. Il a les cheveux noirs et raides et les yeux marron; il fait 1 mètre 78 et pèse 79 kg. Il a une moustache. Il porte un costume bleu marine, une cravate jaune et des chaussures noires.

Look in the Answer key at the back of the book and check that what you've written is correct.

3 **Sally is spending Christmas and New Year in France with a French family. She writes to her friend Isabelle. Complete her letter with the words from the box.**

meilleure longues tout jours confortable prochaine
famille bonnes grande anglaise mieux Chère sympathique

(a) _____ Isabelle,

Je suis depuis une semaine avec la (b) _____ Guise. Ici
(c) _____ le monde est très (d) _____ et je passe de
très (e) _____ vacances. La maison est (f) _____ et
(g) _____. Je fais de (h) _____ promenades presque
tous les (i) _____. La cuisine française est (j) _____
que la cuisine (k) _____ et je mange trop. Je parle
(l) _____ le français maintenant. Je retourne chez
moi la semaine (m) _____.

Joyeux Noël et Bonne Année
Sally

4 **You are in a café with four of your friends.**
The waiter arrives and you order (vous commandez):

Garçon	Bonjour, Messieurs-Dames. Qu'est-ce que vous désirez?
You	*A large black coffee.*
Garçon	Un grand café, oui.
You	*Two draught beers.*
Garçon	Oui.
You	*And a small white coffee.*
Garçon	Alors un grand crème, deux limonades et un petit café noir, c'est ça?
You	*No. Two draught beers, a small white coffee and a large black coffee.*
Garçon	Bon très bien. Excusez-moi.
You	*Have you got some croissants?*
Garçon	Vous_en voulez combien?
You	*Say you want four.*
Garçon	Très bien, Monsieur.

5 **How would you ask for all the items on the list? The words in the box will help, though they aren't all there!**

a a tin of French peas
b an apple tart
c a rum baba
d a vanilla ice cream
e a lemon sorbet
f a white coffee without sugar
g a chicken at 6 € 80
h a cheese sandwich

baba (m)	vanille (f)
petits pois (m)	
pommes (f)	fromage (m)
citron (m)	
sucre (m)	
sandwich (m)	poulet (m)
lait (m)	
tarte (f)	rhum (m)
glace (f)	
café (m)	sorbet (m)
boîte (f)	

Test yourself

1 **Look at the swatches and name the colours in French from top to bottom.**

2 **Unscramble the words to make sentences. Mind the word order with adjectives.**

a c'est/jeune/homme/un/sympathique

_____

b elles/cheveux/longs/ont/et/blonds/les

_____

c ces/noires/sont/lunettes/chères/trop

_____

d mon/ami/habite/vieil/grande/dans/une/ville

_____

3 **Can you say the following?**

a I'd like a tin of green beans.

b A cheese sandwich, please.

c She spends more than I do.

d The book is better than the film.

SELF CHECK

	I CAN...
○	...name colours.
○	...describe things and people.
○	...say precisely what I want.
○	...compare people and objects.

R2 Review 2

This Review covers the main vocabulary and phrases, skills and language points in Units 4–7. You can check your answers in the Answer key.

1 Complete the questions by selecting the appropriate endings.

a	Il y a	1	c'est?
b	Quel âge	2	vous appelez-vous?
c	Qu'est-ce que	3	commencez-vous le matin?
d	À quelle heure	4	ont-ils?
e	Comment	5	une cabine téléphonique près d'ici?

Points: ___ /5

2 Give the opposite of these words and expressions. Mind the masculine, feminine and plural agreements.

a	fermé	f	toujours
b	minuit	g	petit
c	devant	h	femme
d	descendre la rue	i	cheveux courts
e	à gauche	j	nouvelles

Points: ___ /10

3 How would you say and write the following numbers? Mind your French spelling.

a	61 _____	d	94 _____
b	43 _____	e	106 _____
c	80 _____	f	4000 _____

Points: ___ /6

4 Give these times in French using the twenty-four hour clock, then write them down.

Points: ___ /4

5   **Using the example as a model, say these dates in French, then write them out.**

   Example: *Tuesday, the 9th of November:* **le mardi neuf novembre**
   a   Sunday, the 31st of March
   b   Wednesday, the 2nd of June
   c   Friday, the 18th of January
   d   Saturday, the 11th of May
   e   Thursday, the 19th of September

Points: __ /5

6   **You've struck up a conversation with another passenger on the train to Paris. Follow the prompts and take part in the conversation.**

   Man   Vous connaissez déjà Paris?

   You   *Say no. It's the first time you're going there.* (2)

   Man   Et vous restez combien de temps à Paris?

   You   *Say one week.* (1)

   Man   Vous_allez dans_un hôtel?

   You   *Say no. Say you have American friends who live in Paris.* (2)

   Man   Qu'est-ce qu'ils font dans la vie?

   You   *Say he's a journalist and she doesn't work.* (2)

   Man   Ah, c'est bien ... et ils_habitent où à Paris?

   You   *Say they live in the 16th arrondissement, near the Bois de Boulogne.* (2)

   Man   Quelle coincidence. J'habite aussi dans le seizième. Vous prenez_un taxi pour_aller chez vos_amis?

   You   *Say no, taxis are too expensive.* (1)

   Man   Eh bien, ma femme m'attend à la gare avec la voiture. Venez_ avec nous!

   You   Merci beaucoup, Monsieur.

🎧 R2.01 **Listen to the recording to check your answers. Give yourself one or two points for each correct answer, as indicated.**

Points: __ /10
TOTAL __ /40

8 *Vous aimez le sport?*
Do you like sport?

In this unit you will learn how to:
▶ *ask and talk about likes and dislikes.*
▶ *say what you and others do as a hobby.*
▶ *talk about the weather.*
▶ *use **savoir** et **connaître**.*

CEFR: (A2) *can explain personal likes and dislikes, can communicate about hobbies, can describe aspects of the immediate environment such as the weather.*

The most popular sports in France

In France **on aime le sport** (*people like sport*) and **les loisirs** (*pastimes*) often include physical activities. The most popular sports are **le football**, **le tennis**, **l'équitation** (*horse riding*), **le judo** and **la gymnastique** (*gymnastics*).

Ball sports attract more male participants on the whole, although many women and girls can **jouer au golf** (*play golf*) or **jouer au basket** (play basketball) competitively. Water sports have their adepts, and there are plenty of beaches where people can **faire de la natation** (*go swimming*) or **faire de la planche à voile** (*go windsurfing*).

The French **adorent** (*love*) **les sports d'hiver** (*winter sports*) and the skiing resorts in the French Alps enjoy worldwide renown. The February half-term holidays are a time when many French families **vont faire du ski** (*go skiing*).

For the older or less athletic crowd, there are still opportunities to be physically active, perhaps they can **jouer à la pétanque** (*play bowls*) or **faire du vélo** (*go cycling*).

What are the five most popular sports in France?
What is a typical French game of bowls?
Have you noticed which two verbs are used to mean *do* or *play* sports?

76

Vocabulary builder

LES SPORTS *SPORTS*

Qu'est-ce que vous faites comme sport?	*What sport do you do?*
Quels sports pratiquez-vous?	*Which sports do you do?*
Mon sport préféré est la gymnastique.	*Gymnastics is my favourite sport.*
Je fais de la natation.	*I swim.*
J'aime (beaucoup)…	*I like (very much)…*
jouer au squash	*playing squash*
me promener à pied	*going for a walk*
Je joue au tennis.	*I play tennis.*
Je préfère l'équitation.	*I prefer riding.*

LES LOISIRS *HOBBIES*

Vous faites quoi pendant vos loisirs?	*What hobbies do you have?*
Quelle est votre cuisine préférée?	*Which cooking do you prefer?*
la cuisine française	*French cooking*
Je déteste faire la cuisine	*I hate cooking.*
J'adore aller au restaurant.	*I love going to restaurants.*
écouter de la musique	*listening to music*
regarder la télévision	*watching television*
Je n'aime pas…	*I don't like…*
la musique classique	*classical music*
Je joue du piano.	*I play the piano.*

Which French verb is used to speak about hobbies? What's the difference in French between playing sports and playing an instrument?

LE TEMPS *THE WEATHER*

Quel temps fait-il?	*What's the weather like?*
Il fait beau/mauvais.	*The weather is fine/bad.*
Il fait chaud/froid.	*It is hot/cold.*
Le soleil brille.	*The sun shines.*
Il pleut.	*It's raining.*
Il neige.	*It's snowing.*

Conversation

Jane parle de sports et de loisirs avec les Durand. *Jane and the Durands are talking about sport and hobbies.*

08.02 **Listen to the recording or read the dialogue and then answer the questions.**

a What's Mrs Durand's favourite hobby?

b What sports does Mr Durand do?

Jane	Mme Durand, qu'est-ce que vous faites pendant vos loisirs?
Mme Durand	Moi, j'adore faire la cuisine, surtout la cuisine française.
Jane	Et dans la cuisine française, quels sont vos plats favoris?
Mme Durand	Eh bien, j'aime beaucoup faire tous les plats en sauce, en particulier le bœuf bourguignon ou le coq au vin.
Jane	Et vous, Monsieur Durand, vous_aimez faire la cuisine?
M. Durand	Moi, je laisse la cuisine à ma femme. Elle la fait très bien. Je préfère le sport.
Jane	Quels sports pratiquez-vous?
M. Durand	Je joue au squash deux fois par semaine après mon travail et quand j'ai le temps, je fais de la natation avec les_enfants le samedi, à la piscine de Chatou.
Mme Durand	Tu aimes bien aussi faire de la planche à voile en_été.
M. Durand	Oui, c'est vrai. J'aime beaucoup la planche à voile surtout quand_il y a du vent, mais je déteste en faire quand_il fait froid ou quand_il pleut.
Mme Durand	Et vous Jane, qu'est-ce que vous faites comme sport?
Jane	Oh moi, je pratique un peu tous les sports: le badminton, le tennis et quelquefois l'équitation.

c Whose hobby also involves the children?

d Is Jane an accomplished sportswoman? How can you tell?

surtout	*mainly*
plats favoris	*favourite dishes*
le bœuf bourguignon	*beef stew with wine*
le coq au vin	*chicken cooked in wine*
je laisse la cuisine	*I leave the cooking*
elle la fait	*she does it (the cooking)*
quand j'ai le temps	*when I have the time*
en_été	*in summer*
c'est vrai	*it's true*
le vent	*the wind*

Language discovery

1 ASKING AND SAYING WHAT YOU DO AS A HOBBY

In French, to answer questions such as **qu'est-ce que vous faites comme sport?** *what do you do in the way of sport?* or **qu'est-ce que vous faites pendant vos loisirs?** *what are your hobbies?* use **je fais de …** or **je joue à …** if it is a game. If you play a musical instrument, use **je joue de…**

Je fais **de la** natation et **du** surf.	*I swim and I surf.*
Je joue **au** tennis et **à la** pétanque.	*I play tennis and pétanque.*
Je joue **du** piano et **de la** trompette.	*I play the piano and the trumpet.*

How would you say that you do the following: *play the flute, play golf, play badminton, ride horses*? As you answer, mind the masculine and feminine of words.

Je _____ flûte (f).   Je _____ badminton (m).

Je _____ golf (m).   Je _____ équitation (f).

2 LIKES AND DISLIKES

To express your tastes and feelings, you can use **aimer** (*to like, to love*) or the two extremes **adorer** and **détester**:

j'adore	**aller au restaurant**
j'aime (beaucoup)	**jouer au squash**
	la cuisine
	regarder la télé
je n'aime pas	**la musique classique**
	me promener à pied
je déteste	**faire la cuisine**

To say what you like/dislike doing, add the infinitive after **j'aime, j'adore, je déteste, je préfère: je déteste faire de la bicyclette** *I hate cycling.*

How would you say that you like/dislike the following?

jouer du piano (☺)   jouer au golf (☺☺☺)

regarder la télé (☹)   faire des courses (☹☹☹)

Include the article **le**, **la**, **les** when making generalizations:

J'aime les fromages français.   *I like French cheese.*

L'histoire est plus_intéressante   *History is more interesting*
   que la géographie.   *than geography.*

Pratiquez! Practise making generalizations, and remember the articles as you go:

I prefer Italian cooking.   They adore reggae music.

We don't like American films.

3 MORE NEGATIVES

You saw in Unit 3 how to make a statement negative in French, using
ne … pas:

Je **n'**ai pas **d'**enfants.   *I have no children.*

There are other negatives you can use:

ne … plus	*no more/no longer*
ne … rien	*nothing*
ne … jamais	*never*
ne … que	*only*
Je **n'**ai **plus** de vin.	*I have no more wine.*
Il **ne** veut **rien**.	*He wants nothing.*
Il **n'**a **jamais** d'argent.	*He never has any money.*
Je **n'**ai **que** dix_euros.	*I've only got ten euros.*

4 'TO KNOW': WHEN TO USE *SAVOIR*, WHEN TO USE *CONNAÎTRE*

There are two verbs for *knowing*: **savoir** and **connaître**.

a Use **savoir** (on its own) to say that you *know* or *don't know* a fact:

Je sais à quelle heure   *I know when the train leaves.*
   part le train.

Je ne sais pas où est   *I don't know where the bus stop is.*
   l'arrêt d'autobus.

b Use **savoir** followed by the infinitive to say that you know how to do something:

Je sais faire la cuisine.   *I know how to cook.*

Vous savez faire du ski?   *Do you know how to ski?*

c Connaître is used to say that you *know people and places*:

Je connais Paris.	*I know Paris.*
Depuis combien de temps est-ce que vous le connaissez?	*How long have you known him?*

5 QUEL TEMPS FAIT-IL? *WHAT'S THE WEATHER LIKE?*

The easiest way to talk about the weather is to start with **il fait**:

il fait beau, mauvais	*it's fine, the weather is bad*
il fait froid, chaud	*it's cold, hot*
il fait du vent	*it's windy*
il fait du brouillard	*it's foggy*
il fait (du) soleil	*it's sunny*
il pleut	*it's raining*
il neige	*it's snowing*
le soleil brille	*the sun is shining*

How would you answer the question: **Quel temps fait-il aujourd'hui? Aujourd'hui il...**

Practice

1 **Roger Burru has agreed to take part in a survey and is ready to talk about himself. Can you ask him in French the questions on the right?**

a Nom	Roger Burru	*What's your name?*
b Âge	35	*How old are you?*
c Enfants(s)	Non	*Have you any children?*
d Profession	Professeur	*What's your job?*
e Adresse	Lille	*Where do you live?*
f Sport	Natation	*What sport do you do?*
g Loisir	Faire la cuisine	*What are your hobbies?*

08.03 **Now listen to the whole survey and check your answers (or turn to the Answer key).**

Take a turn and answer the same survey questions about yourself.

2 08.04 **Listen carefully as Chloé talks about her likes and dislikes. Then put a tick in the appropriate box:**

	adore	aime beaucoup	n'aime pas	déteste
a Playing volleyball	☐	☐	☐	☐
b Working on Sundays	☐	☐	☐	☐
c Going out in the evenings	☐	☐	☐	☐
d Watching TV	☐	☐	☐	☐
e Listening to music	☐	☐	☐	☐
f Shopping	☐	☐	☐	☐
g Eating out	☐	☐	☐	☐
h Cooking	☐	☐	☐	☐

Now it's your turn to tell Chloé what you like and dislike. Can you think of any more likes/dislikes you could add to the list?

3 Find the right ending for each sentence.

a Il ne va…		**1**	jamais de sport.
b Il n'écoute…		**2**	plus de viande. Il est végétarien.
c Elle ne veut…		**3**	rien faire.
d Il ne mange…		**4**	jamais de musique.
e Elle ne boit…		**5**	plus comme secrétaire.
f Je ne regarde…		**6**	pas dans les musées.
g Il ne fait…		**7**	que de l'eau.
h Elle ne travaille…		**8**	plus la télé.

4 08.05 **Listen to the weather report while looking at the map. Then decide if the statements are (V) vrai or (F) faux.**

a Il fait beau à Newcastle.

b À Brighton, il pleut.

c Il pleut à Calais.

d Le soleil brille à Nice.

e Il pleut à Strasbourg.

f Il fait froid en Espagne.

g Il fait du vent à Malaga.

h Il fait très chaud en Italie.

I Il fait du vent à Rome.

j En Suisse il fait chaud.

k Il neige à Ostende.

l Le soleil brille à Bruxelles.

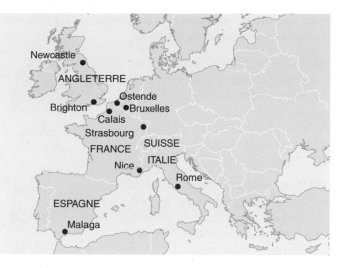

Go further

In this unit, you have seen several uses of **faire de...** to talk about both sports and hobbies. Here are a few more expressions covering popular hobbies for people of all ages.

1 First, match the French and the English.

a	faire de la danse	**1**	to do drama
b	faire des mots croisés	**2**	to do volunteering
c	faire de la peinture	**3**	to do crosswords
d	faire de la photo	**4**	to garden
e	faire du théâtre	**5**	to learn how to dance
f	faire du jardinage	**6**	to paint
g	faire du bénévolat	**7**	to do photography

2 **Read each person's account and note their hobbies. Try to guess the meaning of words you may not know.**

Je m'appelle Marlène et j'ai cinquante-neuf ans. J'aime être active et j'ai beaucoup de loisirs. Je fais de la danse contemporaine deux fois par semaine, mais ma passion c'est le théâtre. Je fais partie d'une troupe de théâtre dans ma banlieue et j'adore ça. Je suis encore trop jeune pour faire des mots-croisés, vous savez.

Mes amis me disent toujours 'Ludovic, tu n'es jamais à la maison'. C'est vrai, je fais beaucoup de sport et mes loisirs prennent tous mes weekends. Je vais au musée des beaux-arts le samedi et je fais de la peinture. Le dimanche, c'est mon jour préféré. Je vais aux rencontres sportives et je fais de la photo en amateur. Souvent, le journal local achète mes photos.

Je m'appelle Séverine et j'habite à Toulouse. Je suis étudiante à l'université. Pendant mes loisirs, je fais du bénévolat au musée des Augustins. C'est un musée d'art classique. Je travaille comme guide avec les touristes et j'adore ça. Je peux parler anglais et espagnol, c'est une bonne expérience.

3 **Use the models above to write about your own hobbies.**

?Test yourself

1 **Say the following in French:**
  a I love playing tennis.
  b Do you like cooking?
  c I don't listen to pop music anymore.
  d I don't know Paris well.
  e She knows how to ski.

2 **Complete the sentences with jouer à... or faire de... changing the form of à or de if required by the noun which follows:**
  a Elle _____ bien _____ tennis.
  b Je _____ l'équitation depuis cinq ans.

c Beaucoup de Français _____ pétanque.

d L'hiver, je _____ ski dans les Alpes.

3 Match the statements and the drawings:

a Il faut du vent.　　　　**1**

b Il fait chaud.　　　　**2**

c Il pleut.　　　　**3**

d Il fait froid.　　　　**4**

Qu'est-ce qu'il faut faire?

What should I do?

In this unit you will learn how to:
- ▶ *ask for assistance.*
- ▶ *give and understand instructions.*
- ▶ *use a few useful linking words.*
- ▶ *use* **pouvoir** *and* **vouloir.**

CEFR: (A2) *Can exchange relevant information and give an opinion on practical problems when asked directly, can respond to suggestions, can understand simple operating instructions.*

Dealing with problems

With foreign travel, it's a fair bet that despite all the careful planning something will go wrong and you will have to solve problems. From simply saying: **je suis perdu, vous pouvez m'aider?** (*I'm lost, can you help me?*), to reporting failures or malfunctions, such as **la machine est en panne** (*the machine is broken down*) or **mon appareil photo ne marche pas** (*my camera is not working*), there are some set phrases you can use to receive assistance.

The French are generally helpful if you show them that you can follow their explanations. Ask questions like **qu'est-ce qu'il faut faire?** (*what must I do?*) or **vous pouvez me dire comment faire?** (*can you tell me what to do?*).

They also appreciate a small show of gratitude for the help they've just given. Saying **merci de votre aide** (*thank you for your help*) will invariably earn you a smile, encouragement and an assurance that it was no trouble, in phrases such as **de rien** (*don't mention it*), **il n'y a pas de quoi** (*there's no need to thank me*), or **je vous en prie** (*it's my pleasure*).

> How would you say that the **distributeur de billets** (*cash point*) is broken down? How about your **portable** (*mobile phone*)?

Vocabulary builder

09.01

DEMANDER DE L'AIDE *ASKING FOR HELP*

Pardon Monsieur, Madame...	*Excuse me...*
Je ne sais pas...	*I don't know...*
Je ne comprends pas...	*I don't understand...*
Vous pouvez m'aider, s'il vous plaît?	*Can you help me please?*
Vous pouvez me montrer comment?	*Can you show me how?*
Qu'est-ce qu'il faut faire?	*What must I/we do?*
Excusez-moi de vous déranger...	*Sorry to disturb you...*

HORS SERVICE *OUT OF SERVICE*

en dérangement	*out of order (machine, telephone)*
La machine ne marche pas.	*The machine does not work.*
en panne	*broken down*

NEW EXPRESSIONS

Il faut_introduire...	*You must insert...*
Vous devez composter le billet.	*You must date-stamp the ticket.*
Je vais m'en_occuper.	*I'll attend to it.*
Ne pas déranger	*Do not disturb.*
d'abord	*firstly*
et puis	*and then*
après ça	*after that*
finalement	*finally*

> What would you say to report a problem with your phone line?
> **Ma ligne (de téléphone) est...**

Conversation

Jane est sur le quai de la gare. Elle essaie de composter son billet pour le valider mais sans succès. Elle arrête une passante.

Jane is on the platform at the station. She is trying to date-stamp her ticket but she is having difficulties. She stops a passer-by.

09.02 Listen and answer the questions.

a What is Jane's problem?

Jane	Pardon, Madame, je ne sais pas comment marche cette machine. Vous pouvez m'aider, s'il vous plaît?
Passante	Mais oui, Mademoiselle, c'est très facile; il faut introduire votre billet sous la flèche verte.
Jane	C'est ce que j'ai fait et ça ne marche pas.
Passante	Alors il faut peut-être tourner le billet dans l'autre sens?
Jane	*(She hears a click.)* Ah, bien, le billet est maintenant composté. Merci, Madame, et excusez-moi de vous avoir dérangée.
Passante	De rien, Mademoiselle.

b What solution does the woman suggest?

la flèche verte *the green arrow*
c'est ce que j'ai fait *that's what I've done*
dans l'autre sens *the other way round*
de rien *don't mention it (lit. for nothing)*

Language discovery

1 ASKING FOR ASSISTANCE

To ask for a favour, start with **vous pouvez** (*can you*) and raise the voice on the last word:

Vous pouvez me montrer, s'il vous plaît? *Can you show me, please?*

Some likely answers:

Oui, avec plaisir. *Yes, with pleasure.*

certainement *certainly*

d'accord *OK*

bien sûr *of course*

Like the verbs **aimer**, **détester**, **adorer** (Unit 8), **vous pouvez** is followed by a verb in the infinitive:

Vous pouvez m'aider, s'il vous plaît? *Can you help me, please?*

Vous pouvez m'accompagner? *Can you come with me?*

How would you ask someone to give you the time? And to speak more slowly?

---

2 TWO VERY USEFUL VERBS: *POUVOIR* (TO BE ABLE TO), *VOULOIR* (TO WANT)

Pouvoir and **vouloir** are two verbs used very frequently in French:

pouvoir to *be able to, can*	vouloir to *want*
je peu**x**	je veu**x**
tu peu**x**	tu veu**x**
il/elle/on peu**t**	il/elle/on veu**t**
nous pouv**ons**	nous voul**ons**
vous pouv**ez**	vous voul**ez**
ils/elles peuv**ent**	ils/elles veul**ent**

As we saw in the examples given above, the most useful form of the verb **pouvoir** is **vous pouvez** followed by **me** and a verb in the infinitive. In the second part of the book there will be many opportunities to use it in everyday situations.

3 GIVING AND UNDERSTANDING INSTRUCTIONS

a The simplest and most commonly used way to give instructions is to use the **vous** or **tu** forms of the present tense:

Pour téléphoner en Grande-Bretagne, **vous composez** le 00, **vous attendez** la tonalité, **vous faites** le 44 puis l'indicatif de la ville sans le 0.

To phone Great Britain, dial 00, wait for the dialling tone, dial 44 then the local code without the zero.

b In written instruction, a verb is often in the infinitive:

Introduire votre billet sous la flèche verte, le **glisser** vers la gauche jusqu'au déclic; si la mention 'tournez votre billet' apparaît, **présenter** l'autre extrémité.

Insert your ticket under the green arrow and slide it to the left until there is a click; if the sign 'turn your ticket' appears, insert the other end.

c **Qu'est-ce qu'il faut…?** To find out what needs to be done, use **qu'est-ce qu'il faut** followed by the appropriate verb in the infinitive:

Qu'est-ce qu'il faut faire pour composter son billet?

What do you have to do to date-stamp your ticket?

d **Il faut** + a verb. Followed by a verb in the infinitive, **il faut** (which is only used in the 3rd person) means any of the following, depending on the context: *it is necessary, I/we/you have to, must, one has to, must*:

Il faut décrocher l'appareil.   *You must lift the receiver.*

Il faut attendre la tonalité.   *You must wait for the dialling tone.*

Il faut composter le billet.   *You must date-stamp your ticket.*

There is another way of saying *must* in French by conjugating the verb **devoir**. Thus you would say: **Je dois composter mon billet** if you say what you must do, and **Vous devez composter votre billet** if you tell someone what he/she must do. Using **Il faut** … is simpler as it applies to everybody.

---

e   Il faut + a noun. Followed by a noun, **il faut** means *you need/one needs/I need.*

Il faut une télécarte pour téléphoner.   *You have to have a phone card to phone.*

Il faut un passeport pour aller en France.   *You must have a passport to go to France.*

Get into the habit of using **Il faut ...** as it is easy to use and very common in France.

How would you say the following in French? *What do you have to do to phone Great Britain? We have to wait for the next train.*

Practice

1   Using the words in the right-hand column, say what is needed in each case. Practise the questions and answers out loud.

Qu'est-ce qu'il faut:

a	pour prendre le train?	**1**	le livre *Get started in French*
b	pour envoyer une lettre?	**2**	une raquette et des balles
c	pour faire une omelette?	**3**	un passeport
d	pour jouer au tennis?	**4**	des_œufs
e	pour jouer de la musique?	**5**	un billet
f	pour apprendre le français?	**6**	un_instrument
g	pour aller en France?	**7**	un timbre

2   Here is a list of things you need to do *to keep fit* pour être en pleine forme. Match them up with the appropriate verbs on the left. You may need to look up some of the words in the vocabulary list at the back of the book.

Pour être en pleine forme il faut:

a	boire	**1**	un sport
b	manger	**2**	les sucreries et le sel
c	pratiquer	**3**	son travail
d	dormir	**4**	peu d'alcool
e	diminuer	**5**	beaucoup de légumes et de fruits
f	aimer	**6**	huit heures par jour

3 Match the two parts of the sentences.

a	Je ne sais pas	1	l'autobus est en panne.
b	Vous pouvez	2	la télé ne marche plus.
c	Je vais au travail à pied,	3	m'expliquer encore une fois?
d	Il faut appeler le réparateur,	4	comment vous aider. C'est trop technique pour moi!

4 Here is a recipe from a children's cookery book. First, match the instructions with the corresponding drawings.

Omelette

(pour quatre personnes)

a D'abord tu bats sept œufs dans un grand bol.

b Puis tu poivres et tu sales.

c Ensuite tu fais fondre dans la poêle 30 grammes de beurre.

d Quand le beurre est chaud, tu verses les œufs.

e Après trois ou quatre minutes, tu mélanges avec une fourchette.

f Finalement, quand l'omelette est cuite, tu sers immédiatement.

5 **Now answer the questions.**

   a How many eggs are needed?

   b What do you do after beating the eggs?

   c What do you melt in the frying pan?

   d When is the egg mixture poured into the frying pan?

   e What do you use to mix the mixture?

6 **To know what to do to read your courriels** *(emails)* **in a French cybercafé, you need to understand some key words and phrases. See if you can put the following lines in a sequential order starting with 1.**

   _____ **a** Donc, il faut appuyer sur le bouton «marche/arrêt».

   _____ **b** et cliquer sur l'Internet avec la souris.

   ___1___ **c** D'abord il faut mettre l'ordinateur en marche.

   _____ **d** et vous pouvez lire vos courriels.

   _____ **e** Finalement vous entrez dans la messagerie,

   _____ **f** Ensuite, il faut aller dans «Menu»,

7 09.03 **You are having difficulty getting your mobile phone to work from France, so you take it to a shop. Take part in the conversation by following the prompts. Listen to the recording to check your answers.**

You	*Say your mobile phone is not working. Ask the man to help you.*
Vendeur	Mais bien sûr. C'est probablement la carte SIM qui ne marche pas en international. C'est_un téléphone anglais?
You	*Say you don't understand and ask the man to speak more slowly.*
Vendeur	D'accord. Il faut changer la carte SIM. Tenez, voici une carte qui marche en France. Vous savez la changer?
You	*Say no, and ask the man to please show you how to do it.*
Vendeur	D'accord. Regardez, c'est très facile.
You	*Thank the man for his help.*
Vendeur	Il n'y a pas de quoi.

Go further

In French there are various ways to say that something should not be done, for example to say that dictionaries aren't allowed during an exam, you can choose between:

Il ne faut pas utiliser de dictionnaire pendant l'examen.

Using a dictionary is forbidden.

Il est interdit d'utiliser un dictionnaire.

Il est défendu d'utiliser un dictionnaire.

Using a dictionary is prohibited.

All three expressions begin with **il** and are followed by a verb. **Il ne faut pas** is meant as a piece of advice or common sense, **Il est interdit** and **il est défendu** are used to talk about rules and what is prohibited by law.

Use the expressions to make sentences with either il ne faut pas, or il est interdit/il est défendu.

a parler pendant le film
b prendre des photos au flash dans le musée
c utiliser son téléphone dans l'avion
d filmer le concert de rock en vidéo
e aller dans l'eau après manger
f nourrir les animaux du zoo

Test yourself

1 How would you say in French?

a I don't know.

_____

b I don't understand.

_____

c Can you help me please?

_____

d The machine does not work.

_____

e What must I do?

_____

f I need a passport to go to France.

_____

g One needs to drink a lot.

_____

2 Unscramble each pair of sentences and give their meaning.

a en / L'autobus / panne / est il / prendre / taxi / faut / un

_____

b D'abord / beurre / fois / le / tu / fondre, les / verses / œufs / tu / et ensuite

_____

c de / Merci / votre / aide Il / de / pas / n'y a / quoi

_____

SELF CHECK

	I CAN. . .
●	. . . ask for assistance.
●	. . . give and understand instructions.
●	. . . use a few useful linking words.
●	. . . use **pouvoir** and **vouloir**.

10 À l'avenir
In the future

In this unit you will learn how to:
- ▶ *say what you usually do.*
- ▶ *say what you need.*
- ▶ *talk about your future plans.*
- ▶ *use the pronoun y.*

CEFR: (A2) *Can use a series of phrases and sentences to describe habits and routines, can use simple language to describe future plans, can make arrangements about where to go and what to do.*

Planning the holidays

In July and August the French **prennent des vacances** (*take a holiday*). Whilst tourists flock to Paris in order to **visiter ses musées et ses monuments** (*visit its museums and monuments*), **les parisiens partent en province** (*Parisians go to France's regions*) or **voyagent à l'étranger** (*travel abroad*). Most families establish a tradition between **aller au bord de la mer** (*go to the seaside*) and **aller à la montagne** (*go to the mountains*).
Visiter les régions (*to visit France's regions*) is high on the agenda, particularly since it is also a way to **rendre visite à la famille et aux amis** (*pay relatives and friends a visit*).

Few French people **restent à la maison** (*stay home*) during the summer holidays, unless it is **la maison de campagne** (*the family country home*).
The summer holidays are never far from people's minds and **où est-ce que vous_allez passer les vacances?** (*where are you going to spend the holidays?*) is a favourite topic of conversation.

What verbs are used in the text to mean *take a holiday* and *spend the holidays*?
In what situations do you think French uses rendre visite à and visiter...?

🎙️ Vocabulary builder

🎧 10.01 **Listen to the speakers talk about their plans then imitate their pronunciation.**

LES PROJETS D'AVENIR *FUTURE PLANS*

demain	*tomorrow*
Qu'est-ce que vous_allez faire?	*What are you going to do?*
Je vais...	*I'm going to...*
rendre visite à mes_amis	*visit my friends*
faire de longues promenades	*to go for long walks*
faire du tourisme	*to do some sightseeing*
sortir (en boîte)	*to go out (to a nightclub)*
passer quelques jours...	*spend a few days...*
partir pour une semaine	*go for a week*
à la campagne	*to the countryside*
Comment passez-vous vos vacances?	*How do you spend your holiday?*
en_été, en_automne, en_hiver	*in summer, in autumn, in winter*
au printemps	*in spring*
l'année prochaine	*next year*
en mars	*in March*
pendant le mois d'août	*during the month of August*

UNE JOURNÉE TYPIQUE *A TYPICAL DAY*

Je me lève.	*I get up.*
Je prends le petit déjeuner.	*I have breakfast.*
Je pars de la maison.	*I leave the house.*
J'emmène les_enfants à l'école.	*I take the children to school.*
Je vais chez mes_amis.	*I go to my friends' house.*
Je fais des courses.	*I do some shopping.*
Je prépare le déjeuner.	*I prepare lunch.*
Je vais chercher Jean à la gare.	*I go and fetch John from the station.*
Le soir, je vais au cinéma.	*In the evening I go to the cinema.*
Je me couche/Je vais au lit.	*I go to bed.*
se baigner	*to go for a swim*
se reposer	*to rest*
lire	*to read*

💡 **What is the difference between je vais chez mes_amis and je vais aller chez mes_amis?**

Conversation

Les Durand parlent de leurs projets pour les 'vacances d'été.

The Durands talk about their summer holiday plans.

 **10.02 Listen and read the conversation at least twice. Then answer the questions.**

a How long are they going on holiday for?

Jane	Monsieur et Madame Durand, qu'est-ce que vous_allez faire pour vos vacances cet_été?
M. Durand	Nous_allons prendre quatre semaines de vacances: une semaine au bord de la mer au mois de juillet et trois semaines à la montagne en_août.
Jane	Vous_allez rester à l'hôtel ou vous_allez louer une maison?
Mme Durand	Nous_allons d'abord passer quelques jours chez nos_amis au bord de la mer. Ils_habitent à 50 km de Nice. Après ça nous_ allons dans notre maison de campagne dans le petit village de Puy-St-Pierre près de Briançon.
Jane	Et comment allez-vous passer vos vacances?
Mme Durand	Au bord de la mer, je vais me baigner tous les jours. À Puy-St-Pierre, je voudrais jouer au tennis, faire de longues promenades et visiter les monuments historiques de la région.
M. Durand	Moi, je vais surtout me reposer, lire et faire un peu de sport comme le tennis ou jouer à la pétanque avec les_enfants. Le soir, j'espère sortir quelquefois pour voir un bon film ou même aller au restaurant.
Rosine	Moi, cette année je ne veux pas faire de tourisme parce que c'est ennuyeux. Je préfère rester à la maison ou sortir avec mes_amis en boîte.

vacances	*holiday* (is always used in the plural form)
louer	*to rent*
surtout	*mostly*
parce que	*because*
ennuyeux	*boring*

b Where are they going?

c Note down at least three things M. and Mme Durand intend to do.

d Does their daughter Rosine enjoy sightseeing?

Language discovery

1 SAYING WHAT YOU USUALLY DO USING SOME REFLEXIVE VERBS

When describing your typical day you can't avoid using reflexive verbs, i.e. verbs describing things you do to or for yourself such as **se lever** (*to get oneself up*), **s'habiller** (*to get dressed*). While in English *myself, yourself, himself*, etc. is often dropped, in French **me, te, se**, etc. must be kept. Here is the pattern followed by all reflexive verbs in the present:

se laver	*to wash (oneself)*
je **me** lave	*I wash (myself)*
tu **te** lav**es**	*you wash (yourself)*
il/elle/on **se** lave	*he/she/it/one washes (himself, etc.)*
nous **nous** lav**ons**	*we wash (ourselves)*
vous **vous** lav**ez**	*you wash (yourself/selves)*
ils/elles **se** lav**ent**	*they wash (themselves)*

Perhaps the most useful reflexive verbs is **s'appeler** (lit. *to call oneself*).

Comment vous_appelez-vous?	**Je m'appelle...**
Comment t'appelles-tu? (friendly form)	**Je m'appelle...**
Comment s'appellent-ils?	**Ils s'appellent...**

> The letter **e** before a single **l** as in **appeler** is always sounded as **e**.
> The letter **e** before a double **ll** as in **appellent** is always sounded as **è**.

Pratiquez! *Practise!* To check that you understand reflexive verbs: try to write out **s'habiller** (*to get dressed*). **Me, te, se** will be shortened to **m', t', s'** as **habiller** starts with an **h**.

2 SAYING WHAT YOU NEED: *J'AI BESOIN DE...*

To say what item you need, use **j'ai besion de** (**d'**) followed by a noun:

J'ai besoin d'un passeport
  pour voyager à l'étranger.

*I need a passport to
  travel abroad.*

Il a besoin d'un timbre
  pour envoyer sa lettre.

*He needs a stamp to
  send his letter.*

To say what you need to do, use **j'ai besoin de** (**d'**) followed by a verb in the infinitive:

J'ai chaud; **j'ai besoin de boire**
  un verre d'eau.

*I'm hot; I need to drink a glass
  of water.*

Elle n'a plus d'argent. **Elle a besoin
  d'aller** à la banque.

*She has no money left. She
  needs to go to the bank.*

J'ai chaud/froid/faim/soif use **avoir** (not **être**).

How would you say: *we are thirsty, are you* **(formal)** *cold? She's
always hungry*.

3 STATING YOUR INTENTIONS

Just as you use **je voudrais** to say what you would like to do, use **je vais** to say what you are going to do followed by the verb in the infinitive:

Je vais	**me lever à huit heures.**
I'm going	*to get up at eight o'clock.*
Tu vas	**prendre le petit déjeuner à neuf heures.**
You're going	*to have breakfast at nine o'clock.*
Il/Elle va	**partir de la maison.**
He/She is going	*to leave the house.*
Nous_allons	**faire des courses à midi.**
We're going	*to do some shopping at lunchtime.*
Vous_allez	**chercher Jean à la gare.**
You're going	*to fetch John from the station.*
Ils/Elles vont	**se coucher vers 11 heures.**
They're going	*to go to bed around 11 o'clock.*

Instead of the future tense you can also use the present if it is accompanied by a word which indicates that the action will take place in the future. Thus you can say: **je prends le train demain** instead of **je vais prendre le train demain.**

4 THE PRONOUN Y

To replace an expression of place preceded by **à**, use the pronoun **y** (*there*), which comes right before the verb:

Vous_allez à Paris?	*Are you going to Paris? Yes, I'm*
Oui, j'y vais.	*going there.*
Tu vas au cinéma demain?	*Are you going to the cinema tomorrow?*
Oui, j'y vais.	*Yes, I am (going there).*
Vous venez souvent au bord de la mer?	*Do you often come to the seaside?*
Oui, nous_y venons régulièrement.	*Yes, we come here regularly.*

5 USING CAPITAL LETTERS

The months and days of the week do not take a capital letter in French unless they begin a sentence (Unit 5): **en juillet**, **le mardi**.

6 WHEN TO USE *VISITER* (TO VISIT) IN FRENCH

French people talk about visiting museums, old buildings or interesting places but they do not visit the cinema or their relations! They go to the cinema or the pub and they pay a visit or see their relations or friends:

Je vais_aller visiter le Louvre l'été prochain.	*I'm going to visit the Louvre next summer.*
Ce week-end je vais rendre visite à ma grand-mère.	*This weekend I'm going to visit my grandmother.*
Ils vont voir leurs_amis dans le sud de la France.	*They are going to visit their friends in the south of France.*

Practice

1 **Find the right ending for each sentence.**

a Est-ce que vous **aimez**   1 tes vacances?

b ils vont passer **une**   2 faire de longues promenades?

c En juillet, je vais **voyager**   3 un mois à la montagne.

d Comment passes-**tu**   4 semaine à la campagne.

e Qu'est-ce que nous **allons**   5 à l'étranger.

f Mes amis **passent**   6 faire demain?

2 **How would you say the following in French?**

a I get up at 8 o'clock.

b We're going to go for a swim this afternoon.

c They have breakfast at the hotel.

d In July she spends three weeks at the seaside.

e Are you going to rent a house?

3 Imagine this is your typical day. Look at the pictures and have a go at saying what you do during the day. Then try to write it out.

a D'abord je …

b puis je …

c ensuite …

d À 8h.30 j'…

e ensuite …

f à midi …

g L'après-midi …

h ou je …

i ou je …

j Le soir je …

k ou j'…

l enfin …

4 Your friends Robert and Jeanine have just planned their holidays for this summer. You ask them about it:

  a What does Robert say?

  b What does Jeanine tell you?

	Robert	Jeanine
Tu va partir quand?	in August	on 21st June
Pour combien de temps?	three weeks	ten days
Comment vas-tu passer tes vacances?	visit old buildings see some friends go out in the evening play tennis	read a lot watch a bit (**un peu**) of TV go for long walks go to bed early (**tôt**)

Practise the exercise several times and try memorizing the questions.

5 Jane has received an email from Christine, a French friend who is about to visit her in Brighton. Complete the email using the words in the box.

> prendre fils Grande-Bretagne jours
> finit samedi rester visiter besoin

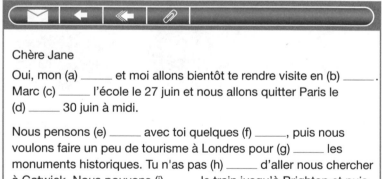

Chère Jane

Oui, mon (a) _____ et moi allons bientôt te rendre visite en (b) _____.
Marc (c) _____ l'école le 27 juin et nous allons quitter Paris le
(d) _____ 30 juin à midi.

Nous pensons (e) _____ avec toi quelques (f) _____, puis nous
voulons faire un peu de tourisme à Londres pour (g) _____ les
monuments historiques. Tu n'as pas (h) _____ d'aller nous chercher
à Gatwick. Nous pouvons (i) _____ le train jusqu'à Brighton et puis
un taxi jusqu'à chez toi.

À très bientôt
Christine

6 Change the following sentences by replacing the highlighted words with **y**. Remember to pay attention to the word order.
   a Je travaille à la banque.
   b Ils ne vont jamais au restaurant.
   c Vous allez à la montagne en hiver?
   d Nous allons souvent aux matches de football.

Listening and speaking

1 10.03 Michel has a lot of things planned for tomorrow. Listen to the recording to find out what's he's going to do. He has a list of seven things. Make a note of Michael's plans, then check the answers in the Answer key.

2 Now it is your turn to tell Michel about your next holiday. Answer his questions according to the prompts – and pretend you're a married man if you have to!

Michel	Quest-ce que vous allez faire pour vos vacances cet été?
You	*You're going to go to Portugal.*
Michel	Vous_y allez seul ou avec votre famille?
You	*With your wife and your two children.*
Michel	Quand partez-vous_au Portugal?
You	*You're going during the month of August.*
Michel	Et vous_y resterez combien de temps?
You	*You're going to spend two weeks at the seaside.*
Michel	Et comment allez-vous passer vos vacances?
You	*The children will play tennis in the mornings and swim in the afternoons.*
Michel	Et vous et votre femme, qu'allez-vous faire pendant la journée?
You	*You're going to rest and take walks.*
Michel	Et le soir?
You	*You're going to read or speak with your friends.*
Michel	Et les_enfants? Ils vont sortir le soir?
You	*Yes, they can go out clubbing (**sortir en boîte**) with their friends.*

10.04 Now listen to the dialogue to check your answers.

Go further

Sortir and **venir** are two useful verbs to describe daily activities:

sortir *to go out*	**venir** *to come*
je sor**s**	je vien**s**
tu sor**s**	tu vien**s**
il/elle/on sor**t**	il/elle/on vien**t**
nous sort**ons**	nous ven**ons**
vous sort**ez**	vous ven**ez**
ils/elles sort**ent**	ils/elles vienn**ent**

Sortir is used in the sense of leaving somewhere:

Je sors du cinéma.

Elles sortent du magasin.

It's also used in the sense of going out:

Tu veux sortir avec moi ce soir?

In French **aller** and **venir** indicate the point of view of the speaker:

Vous allez souvent à la montagne? (I am asking but I'm not there now)

Vous venez souvent à la montagne? (I am asking and I'm there now)

In questions, **venir** is often used as an invitation to go along:

Tu viens au ciné? *Do you want to come to the cinema?*

1 **Complete the sentences with the correct form of the verb in brackets.**
   a Ce soir, nous _____ (sortir) au restaurant.
   b Tu _____ (venir) au concert demain?
   c Elles _____ (sortir) très souvent avec des amis.
   d Nous _____ (venir) en vacances ici tous les étés.
   e Pendant les vacances, sa mère _____ (venir) en visite.
   f Il _____ (sortir) en boîte ou au cinéma avec sa petite amie.
   g Et vous _____ (venir) souvent à Marseille?
   h J'ai besoin de _____ (sortir) tôt aujourd'hui.

2 **Describe one of your typical days. Use some or all of the words in the list.**

| se lever   partir de la maison   aller travailler |
| déjeuner   rendre visite à   faire des courses |
| sortir avec des amis   regarder la télé   se coucher |

? Test yourself

Say the following in French.

a We get up at seven o'clock in the morning.

_____

b She's going to visit London's monuments.

_____

c I need to buy the newspaper.

_____

d How will you spend your holiday? (familiar)

_____

e In the summer we visit our grandparents.

_____

f I'm going out with my friends.

_____

SELF CHECK

	I CAN...
⚪	. . . say what I usually do.
⚪	. . . say what I need.
⚪	. . . talk about future plans.
⚪	. . . use the pronoun **y.**

You have finished the first part of the book with the basic structures and grammatical points. Before going on to the second part of the course which deals with everyday situations, do Review 3 (Units 8–10). Check your written answers in the Answer key then record your score in the box provided after the test.

Review 3

This test Review covers the main vocabulary and phrases, skills and language points in Units 8–10. **Bonne chance!**

1 Look at the chart below and report on the likes and dislikes of two friends, Sophie et Mohamed.

	Sophie	Mohamed
a playing football	☹	☺
b cooking	☺	☹
c watching TV	☺	😐
d listening to music	❤	☺
e swimming	😐	❤
f skiing	❤	☹
g going to restaurants	😐	☺
h playing tennis	☹	❤

déteste	n'aime pas	aime beaucoup	adore
☹	😐	☺	❤

Points: __ /16

2 Complete the missing part of the reflexive verbs.

a je _____ lève

b tu _____ habilles

c il _____ lave

d nous _____ baignons

e vous _____ reposez

f elles _____ couchent

Points: __ /6

3 Can you think of the right verb (in the correct form) to complete the sentences?

a Je n'_____ que de la musique classique.

b Tu _____ de la viande. Tu n'es pas végétarienne.

c Nous _____ comme secrétaires.

d Vous _____ du piano et de la flûte.

e En France, on _____ beaucoup de sports.

Points: __ /5

4　Talk about the weather in France, incorporating each icon on the map below into a full sentence, for example: **chaud → il fait chaud**.

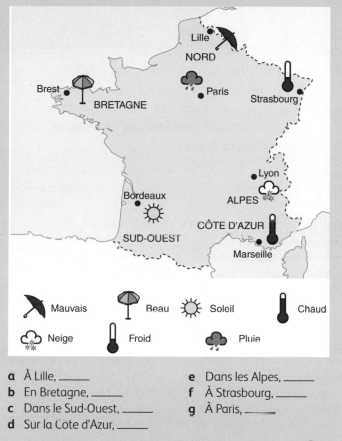

a　À Lille, _____
b　En Bretagne, _____
c　Dans le Sud-Ouest, _____
d　Sur la Côte d'Azur, _____

e　Dans les Alpes, _____
f　À Strasbourg, _____
g　À Paris, _____

Points: ___ /7

5　**Complete the sentences with aller + verb to talk about future plans.**
a　Qu'est-ce que vous _____ faire pour vos vacances?
b　Nous _____ passer deux semaines de vacances au bord de la mer.
c　Jane _____ visiter le sud de la France.
d　Tu _____ aller voir le film ce soir?
e　Je _____ me reposer chez moi.
f　Les Durand _____ se baigner tous les jours

Points: ___ /6

6   Choose the right verbs to write the email.

| rendre | se baigner | sortir | faire | se promener | passer |

Salut de Bretagne! Je **(a)** _____ quelques jours au bord de la mer.

Je **(b)** _____ sur la plage le matin, et je **(c)** _____ l'après-midi.

Le soir, je **(d)** _____ au cinéma avec les copains. Demain je vais

(e) _____ visite à ma tante qui habite Nantes. Nous allons

(f) _____ du tourisme dans la ville.

A bientôt,

Points: ___ /6

7   Match the expressions in bold with their meaning.

a   Le train est en panne.   1   out of order
b   Ma montre ne marche pas.   2   no longer works
c   Mon assiette est cassée.   3   broken down
d   Le téléphone est en dérangement.   4   isn't working
e   La machine à café ne marche plus.   5   is broken

Points: ___ /6

8   Unscramble the sentences to reveal the instructions for booking cinema tickets online. Give yourself two points for each correct sentence.

a   sélectionner / D'abord / un / il / faut / film.
b   l'heure / ça / il / choisir / film. / faut / du / Après
c   de / nombre / Troisièmement / le / indiquer / personnes. / doit / on
d   cliquer / Ensuite / faut / 'acheter'. / il / sur
e   insérer / Puis / numéro de / doit / son / carte bancaire. / on
f   faut / le / Et finalement, il / noter / confirmation. / numéro de

Points: ___ /12

9   Say what action you need to take in each situation. Use **j'ai besoin de...**, and the words in brackets.

Example: Je voyage aux USA (passeport) → J'ai besoin d'obtenir un passeport.

a   J'ai chaud. (boire / eau)
b   Je voudrais quitter le restaurant. (demander / addition)

c Je n'ai plus d'argent. (aller / banque)

d J'ai froid. (mettre / vêtement chaud)

e J'ai le soleil dans les yeux. (porter / lunettes de soleil)

f J'ai faim. (manger / snack)

Points: __ /6

10 R3.01 **You invited some French friends to come and stay with you. Eva phones you to arrange their visit. Follow the prompts and take part in the conversation. Give yourself one or two points for each correct answer, as indicated.**

Eva   Allô, c'est Eva ici. Lionel et moi aimerions vous rendre visite pour nos vacances. Vous pouvez nous recevoir cet été?

You   *Say you don't speak French very well. Ask her to speak more slowly.* (2)

Eva   Est-ce que nous pouvons rester chez vous pendant le mois d'août?

You   *Ask when they want to come during the month August?* (1)

Eva   Nous souhaitons venir du 1er au 15 août.

You   *Say you're really sorry, but you cannot in August.* (2)

Eva   Ah quel dommage!

You   *Say that you are in Canada from 20 July through 20 August.* (1)

You   *Say you would really like to see them. Ask if they can change the dates of their holiday?* (2)

Eva   Si vous préférez, on peut venir au début du mois de septembre?

You   *Say that these dates work better for you.* (1)

Eva   Alors c'est parfait. Je peux prendre le billet pour septembre?

You   *Say yes, she can purchase the ticket.* (1)

Points: __ /10

TOTAL __ /80

60–80 points	Congratulations! Your French is great.
50–59 points	Very good. You have good control of the language covered in the course.
36–49 points	Well done, but look at your detailed scores and revise the language that gives you problems
35 points or less	Not bad, but you will benefit from reviewing Units 1–10.

11 Les courses
Shopping

In this unit you will learn how to:
▶ *find the right French shop for what you need.*
▶ *buy groceries.*
▶ *shop for something to wear.*

Before you start, revise:
▶ *numbers (Units 1–6).*
▶ *some and any (Unit 2, Section 3).*
▶ *asking the price (Unit 2, Section 5).*
▶ *saying precisely what you want (Unit 7, Section 2).*
▶ *more and less (Unit 7, Section 4).*
▶ *colours (Unit 7, The meaning of colours).*

Les magasins en France

Les magasins, en France, restent ouverts en général jusqu'à 19 heures ou 20 heures. Beaucoup ferment entre 12 heures et 14 heures. Le lundi ils sont souvent fermés dans les petites villes.

La **boulangerie** (*baker's*), ouvre très tôt, vers sept heures du matin, et ferme tard car beaucoup de Français achètent leur pain deux fois par jour. Le dimanche matin, beaucoup de magasins comme les pâtisseries et les charcuteries restent ouverts.

Dans toutes les grandes villes il y a un marché presque tous les jours et souvent le dimanche. Dans les petites villes ou villages il y a un marché une fois par semaine: le jour du marché. Au marché, on peut acheter des **légumes** (*vegetables*), des fruits, du **poisson** (*fish*), de la **viande** (*meat*) et même des **vêtements** (*clothes*).

1 **Answer the questions to help you understand the passage about French shops.**

   a Until what time do shops generally stay open during the week?
   b Are they usually open or shut at lunchtime?
   c What day of the week do they often shut?
   d Which shops stay open on Sunday morning?

The difference between **une charcuterie** *delicatessen* and **une boucherie** *butcher's* is simple. A **charcuterie** sells cooked meats such as salami and pâté, while a **boucherie** sells uncooked meats such as pork chops and sausages.

🎙 Vocabulary builder

ACHETER DES PROVISIONS *FOOD SHOPPING*

🎧 11.01 **Listen to the new vocabulary and imitate the pronunciation of the speakers.**

À la boucherie on achète:

du veau	*veal*
du bœuf	*beef*
du porc	*pork*
des saucisses	*sausages*
du poulet	*chicken*

À la charcuterie on achète:

du jambon	*ham*
du saucisson	*salami-type sausage*

À la boulangerie/pâtisserie on achète:

un pain complet	*wholemeal loaf*
une tarte aux fraises	*strawberry tart*
des croissants	*croissants*

À l'épicerie (*grocer's*), **à l'alimentation** (*foodstore*), **au supermarché**
(*supermarket*) **on achète:**

du thé	*tea*
du café	*coffee*
du beurre	*butter*
du lait	*milk*
des œufs (rhyming with **deux**)	*eggs*
du fromage (de chèvre)	*(goat's) cheese*
du dentifrice	*toothpaste*
des pommes	*apples*
des pommes de terre	*potatoes*
des yaourts à la pêche	*peach yoghurts*
des boissons (jus de fruit, vins, etc.)	*drinks (fruit juice, wine, etc.)*

2 **There is no supermarket around; say in French which shops sell:**
 a chicken
 b wholemeal bread
 c pork
 d toothpaste
 e milk
 f salami
 g wine

3 **Here is a dialogue between a grocer and a client. See if you can put the lines in their correct order starting with 1.**
 _____ **a** Une douzaine (a dozen), s'il vous plaît.
 _____ **b** Voilà, Madame, ça fait 6€85.
 __1__ **c** Bonjour Madame.
 _____ **d** Non, il me faut aussi du jus de fruit.
 _____ **e** Oui … voilà une douzaine d'œufs, c'est tout?
 _____ **f** Bonjour Monsieur, je voudrais des œufs, s'il vous plaît.
 __7__ **g** Qu'est-ce que je vous donne: jus de pomme, orange ou ananas (*pineapple*)?
 _____ **h** Vous en voulez combien?
 _____ **i** Je vais prendre le jus d'orange.

NEW EXPRESSIONS

11.02 Listen to the new expressions and try to memorize them.

Où est la boulangerie la plus proche, s'il vous plaît?	*Where is the nearest bakery please?*
Où est le supermarché le plus proche?	*Where is the nearest supermarket?*
Où est-ce que je peux acheter/trouver un/une/des…	*Where can I buy/find a/some…*
Je voudrais/Il me faut…	*I would like/I need…*
Je vais prendre une tranche/un kilo/une livre de plus.	*I'll take a slice/a kilo/a pound more.*
500 grammes de moins	*500 grams less*
un demi-kilo	*half a kilo*
un paquet/une plaquette de…	*a pack of…*
une tranche de…	*a slice of…*
un morceau de…	*a piece of…*

 How would you say *Where is the closest grocer's?*

DANS LES MAGASINS *IN THE SHOPS*

On s'occupe de vous?	*Are you being served?*
Et avec ceci (ça)?	*Is that all?* (lit. *And with this?*)
Je cherche quelque chose de différent.	*I'm looking for something different.*
Vous avez quelque chose de plus… grand/petit/moins cher?	*Have you got anything bigger/smaller/ cheaper?*
Vous avez autre chose?	*Do you have anything else?*
C'est tout, merci.	*That's all, thank you.*
C'est trop grand/petit/cher.	*It's too big/small/expensive.*

 How would you say *I'm looking for something smaller?*

Conversation

Au marché, un client achète des provisions pour un pique-nique.

At the market a customer buys some food for a picnic.

🎧 4 11.03 **Listen to the conversation and answer the questions.**

   a What does the client buy for dessert?

Client	Bonjour, mademoiselle. Je voudrais du beurre, s'il vous plaît.
Vendeuse	Une plaquette comme ça?
Client	Non, quelque chose de plus petit. Et qu'est-ce que vous avez comme fromages?
Vendeuse	Brie, fromage de chèvre, gruyère. Qu'est-ce que je vous donne?
Client	Du gruyère.
Vendeuse	Un morceau comme ça?
Client	Ah non … ça c'est un peu trop gros. Vous pouvez m'en donner un peu moins, s'il vous plaît? C'est pour notre pique-nique.
Vendeuse	Ah bon, d'accord. Voilà … 300 grammes. Et avec ça? Qu'est-ce qu'il vous faut? Des fruits, des yaourts, des biscuits?
Client	Euh, je vais prendre aussi des fruits.
Vendeuse	Alors nous avons des fraises, des bananes, des pommes, des pêches et du melon.
Client	Elles sont bonnes les fraises?
Vendeuse	Délicieuses. Je vous en mets un demi-kilo?
Client	500 grammes! Non, c'est un peu trop. Une demi-livre c'est assez. Ah oui, je voudrais aussi deux grandes bouteilles d'eau minérale … Voilà, c'est tout, c'est combien?
Vendeuse	Alors, ça vous fait 19€83.
Client	Et pour acheter du pain?
Vendeuse	Vous trouverez une boulangerie à 200 mètres sur votre gauche. Et … bon pique-nique Monsieur.

   b What does he buy to drink?
   c What expressions does he use to mean *it's a bit too big* and *it's enough*?

5 Look at the words below. Can you pick out four items bought by the customer?

a du poulet   e des pommes   i du lait
b du beurre   f du melon   j du vin
c du saucisson   g des fraises   k de la bière
d du fromage   h des pêches   l de l'eau minérale

6 Pretend that you're a customer. Use the conversation and the Vocabulary builder to practise buying the following items. Say:

a I'd like 300 grams of cheese.
b I'll take a half a pound of strawberries.
c Can you give me a packet of ham?
d That's all. How much is it?

7 Here is a list of some shops and services in the town of Cauterets.

Alimentation Générale – Primeurs – **Ets. Vaud**
Bijouterie – **Angélique**
Brasserie – **«Au bon accueil»**
Boucherie – Charcuterie – **Bon et fils**
Cave – Marchand de Vin – **Veuve de Bonnet**
Chaussures – **Saint-Etienne**
Droguerie – **Sans souci**
Informatique – **infocom**
Librairie – *Blanchard*
Lingerie – Vêtements – **«Chez Madame»**
Pressing – **À votre service**

Can you identify the French words for:

a dry-cleaner's
b book shop/store
c IT
d jewellery
e shoe shop
f ladies' wear
g delicatessen
h off-licence

Vocabulary builder

À LA DROGUERIE *HARDWARE SHOP*

une brosse à dent	*toothbrush*
un savon	*soap*
un peigne	*comb*
de l'huile pour bronzer	*suntan lotion*
des kleenex	*tissues*
un ouvre-boîte	*tin opener*
un tire-bouchon	*corkscrew*

AU BUREAU DE TABAC *NEWSAGENT'S*

un carnet de timbres	*book of stamps*
des journaux	*newspapers*
du chewing gum	*chewing gum*
une carte postale	*postcard*
des magazines	*magazines*

AU MAGASIN DE VÊTEMENTS *CLOTHES SHOP*

un pull-over	*pullover*
un pantalon	*trousers*
une chemise	*shirt*
une paire de chaussures	*shoes*
un maillot de bain	*swimming costume*
une robe	*dress*
une jupe	*skirt*
un jean/des jeans	*jeans*

8 **Look back at the vocabulary and find the appropriate item for each of these situations.**

   a Pour ouvrir une bouteille, il faut _____ .

   b Il faut mettre _____ pour faire de la natation.

   c Avant d'aller au soleil, il faut mettre de _____ .

   d Pour lire les nouvelles du jours, il faut acheter les _____ .

   e On met le dentifrice sur une _____ .

Conversation

This dialogue takes place in **un magasin de vêtements** and includes some new questions you will need to understand:

Quelle taille?   *What size?* (42 is the European equivalent to the woman's size 14 in Britain and 12 in America)

Quelle pointure?   *What shoe size?*

Je peux essayer?   *Can I try it on?*

11.04 **Listen to a woman who is looking for a specific skirt to buy. Then, do the next activity to check your understanding.**

Cliente	Bonjour, Madame, je cherche une jupe noire.
Vendeuse	Noire … euh oui d'accord. Vous faites quelle taille?
Cliente	40 … 40/42, ça dépend du modèle.
Vendeuse	J'ai ce modèle-ci en 40 et 42. C'est une jupe en coton. En 40, je n'ai pas de noir; j'ai du rouge, du gris mais pas de noir.
Cliente	Elles font combien ces jupes?
Vendeuse	63€.
Cliente	Vous n'avez pas quelque chose de moins cher?
Vendeuse	Euh non, sauf ces jupes en solde à 47€ mais elles sont grises.
Cliente	Non, il me faut du noir. Bon, eh bien, je vais essayer la jupe à 63€.
Vendeuse	*(pointing to a changing room)* Vous avez la cabine d'essayage là-bas.
After a while...	
Vendeuse	Elle vous va bien?
Cliente	Ça va; elle est un peu large mais je crois que je vais la prendre car j'en ai besoin pour ce soir. Vous acceptez les cartes de crédit?
Vendeuse	Mais bien sûr, Madame.

9 **How well did you follow the conversation? Match the French and the English.**

a vous faites quelle taille?   1 on sale
b ça dépend du modèle   2 fitting room
c en solde   3 over there
d la cabine d'essayage   4 it depends on the style
e là-bas   5 what size are you?

10 **Listen to the audio again and try to spot the French version of the following phrases, then write them down:**

a I'm looking for a black skirt.
b How much are these skirts?
c something cheaper
d Do you accept credit cards?

11 **You're at the bureau de tabac (the c in tabac is not sounded) and wish to buy a newspaper, stamps, cards and a magazine for your wife. Follow the prompts and take part in the conversation.**

Vendeur	Bonjour, Monsieur, vous désirez?
You	*Say you would like a newspaper. Ask him what English newspapers he's got.*
Vendeur	Comme journaux anglais? Nous avons le *Times*, le *Guardian* et le *Daily Telegraph*.
You	*Say that you will take* The Times *and these three postcards. Ask how much a stamp for England is.*
Vendeur	Un timbre pour l'Angleterre? C'est 77 centimes.
You	*Say that you will take eight stamps.*
Vendeur	Voilà, Monsieur; huit timbres à 77 centimes. C'est tout?
You	*Say that you'll also buy the magazine* Elle *for your wife.*
Vendeur	Très bien, Monsieur. Ça vous fait 15€85.

12 11.05 **Listen to Michel who's out clothes shopping. Listen to the conversation several times and then answer the questions in English.**

a What does he want to buy?
b What colours does he ask for?
c What's wrong with the first garment?
d What's wrong with the second garment?
e How much is the one he buys?

? Test yourself

1 Match the two parts of the sentences and give their meaning.

a	Vous faites	**1**	dix tranches de jambon.
b	Vous n'avez pas	**2**	la cabine d'essayage?
c	Où se trouve	**3**	de vous, Messieurs-dames?
d	je vais prendre	**4**	quelle taille?
e	On s'occupe	**5**	quelque chose de différent?

2 Complete the sentences with the appropriate word.

a Où est-ce que je peux trouver/acheter une épicerie?

b Où est la boulangerie la plus proche/ouverte?

c Je cherche quelque/une chose de moins cher.

d Je vais prendre une douzaine de beurre/d'œufs aussi.

e Je voudrais une plaquette de beurre/saucisson.

3 In each series, there is a word that doesn't belong. Can you spot it?

a veau, jambon, lait, saucisson, poulet

b melon, fraise, pomme de terre, pêche, banane

c fromage, lait, yaourt, beurre, pain

SELF CHECK

I CAN...
○ ... find the right French shop for what I need.
○ ... buy groceries.
○ ... shop for something to wear.

12 Se reposer, dormir
Resting, sleeping

In this unit you will learn how to:
- ▶ *ask for information at the tourist office.*
- ▶ *book into a hotel.*
- ▶ *complain about things missing/not working.*
- ▶ *spell your name.*
- ▶ *book accommodation online.*

Before you start, revise:
- ▶ *saying precisely what you want (Unit 7, Section 2).*
- ▶ *different ways to ask a question (Unit 5, Section 3).*
- ▶ *asking the price (Unit 2, Section 5).*
- ▶ *recognizing 'first', 'second', 'third', etc. (Unit 6, Section 8).*
- ▶ *saying there is, there are (Unit 4, Section 4).*
- ▶ *dates (Unit 5, Section 4).*

À l'hôtel

Les hôtels sont **homologués** (*classified*) par le gouvernement qui utilise un système d'**étoiles** (*stars*). Les hotels simples ont une étoile * (hôtel simple) et les **hôtels de luxe** (*luxury hotels*) cinq étoiles **** (très grand confort, palace). Tous doivent **afficher** (*display*) leurs **prix TTC** (toutes taxes comprises) à l'extérieur de l'hôtel et dans les chambres. Les chambres proposent en général un lit à deux personnes ou deux lits à une personne. On a généralement le choix entre pension complète et demi-pension. Il faut demander si le petit déjeuner est compris dans le prix de la chambre. Il est souvent en supplément. Il existe encore en France une grande tradition d'hôtels restaurants, où l'on peut trouver de très bonnes tables.

 How would you filter the hotels on a French web page if you wanted to only research budget hotels?
What acronym is used in the passage to mean *price after tax?*
What expression is used to mean *very good restaurants?*

Vocabulary builder

12.01

TROUVER OÙ SE LOGER *FINDING ACCOMMODATION*

je cherche …	*I'm looking for …*
un logement	*accommodation*
un appartement	*a flat/apartment*
un gîte rural	*a self-catering cottage*
à louer	*to rent*
meublé et équipé	*furnished and fully equipped*
rester chez l'habitant	*to stay as a paying guest*

FAIRE UNE RÉSERVATION *BOOKING ACCOMMODATION*

Vous avez…?	*Have you…?*
une chambre de libre	*a vacancy*
une chambre d'hôte	*a room in a guest house*
Je voudrais réserver…	*I would like to book …*
une chambre simple/double	*a single/double room*
à deux lits	*with two single beds*
avec un grand lit	*with a double bed*
avec douche et WC	*with shower and WC*
avec salle de bains	*with bathroom*
avec pension complète	*with full board*
avec demi-pension	*with half board*
pour deux personne(s)	*for two person(s)*
pour trois nuit(s)	*for three night(s)*
du … au	*from … to*
Le petit déjeuner est compris?	*Is breakfast included?*
C'est en supplément/en plus.	*It's extra.*
C'est à quel nom?	*In whose name?*
la caution	*deposit*
C'est complet.	*It's full up.*

Go over the list and find the three different types of accommodation that are listed.

1 12.02 **Study the following icons. They describe the type of services offered in a four-star hotel and room. Find the matching explanation for each icon then listen to the recording to check your answers.**

a

b

c

d

e £ $ €

f

g ℗

h

i

j

k

l

m

n

o

p WiFi

1 Climatisation _____

2 Accès handicapé _____

3 Mini-bar _____

4 Bureau de change dans l'hôtel _____

5 Service en chambre _____

6 Bagagiste _____

7 Sèche-cheveux _____

8 Navette aéroport _____

9 Coffre-fort _____

10 Chambre non-fumeur _____

11 Piscine _____

12 Ascenseur _____

13 Télévision via satellite _____

14 Animaux acceptés _____

15 WiFi _____

16 Parking privé _____

Conversation

À LA RECHERCHE D'UN HÔTEL *LOOKING FOR A HOTEL*

À l'office du tourisme une touriste et son mari se renseignent sur les hôtels à Paris.

At the tourist office, a tourist and her husband enquire about hotels in Paris.

2 12.03 **Listen to the conversation and answer the questions.**

a What's the tourist's concern regarding the hotel?

Touriste	Bonjour Madame. Je viens d'arriver à Paris et je cherche une chambre. Vous avez une liste d'hôtels, s'il vous plaît?
Hôtesse	Oui Madame, voilà.
The tourists look at the brochure.	
Touriste	Vous pouvez me réserver une chambre, s'il vous plaît?
Hôtesse	Oui, bien sûr. Vous choisissez quel hôtel?
Touriste	Un hôtel à trois étoiles, l'Hôtel Victor Hugo, dans le 16ème arrondissement.
Hôtesse	C'est pour combien de personnes?
Touriste	Euh, pour mon mari et moi.
Hôtesse	Et pour combien de nuits?
Touriste	Pour deux nuits.
Hôtesse	Bien. Une chambre à deux lits ou un grand lit?
Touriste	Un grand lit. Nous voulons aussi une douche ou une salle de bains dans la chambre.
Hôtesse	Bon, alors une chambre pour deux nuits, pour deux personnes avec un grand lit et douche ou salle de bains. Très bien, je vais téléphoner et je vous réserve ça tout de suite.
Touriste	J'espère que l'hôtel n'est pas complet!
Hôtesse	Je crois qu'en cette saison, il y a des chambres de libre.

b How long does the tourist couple intend to stay at the hotel Victor Hugo?

c What expression does the **hôtesse** use to mean she'll book the room right away?

> Paris is divided into 20 **arrondissements**, or *administrative districts*.

Conversation

À L'HÔTEL *IN THE HOTEL*

À la réception: les Wilson arrivent à leur hôtel.
At reception: the Wilsons arrive at their hotel.

3 12.04 **Listen and answer the questions.**

a **What is included in the price of the room?**

Touriste	Bonjour, Monsieur. Nous avons une réservation au nom de Wilson.
Réceptionniste	Ah oui, vous êtes les Anglais qui ont téléphoné cet après-midi!
Touriste	Oui, c'est ça.
Réceptionniste	Bon, vous avez la chambre 43 au deuxième étage. C'est une chambre très agréable avec grand lit, douche et WC.
Touriste	Le petit déjeuner est compris dans le prix de la chambre?
Réceptionniste	Ah non, Madame, c'est en plus: sept euros par personne.
Touriste	Et à quelle heure servez-vous le petit déjeuner?
Réceptionniste	À partir de 7.30 heures jusqu'à 10 heures.
Touriste	Vous servez le petit déjeuner dans la chambre?
Réceptionniste	Mais oui, Madame, bien sûr.
Touriste	Très bien. Pouvez-vous nous apporter demain matin le petit déjeuner à 8.30, s'il vous plaît?
Réceptionniste	C'est entendu, Madame.
Touriste	Est-ce qu'il y a un ascenseur dans l'hôtel? Nos valises sont très lourdes.
Réceptionniste	Oui, au fond du couloir à droite.

b Does the hotel offer room service?

c What are the breakfast hours?

4 **Read or listen to the conversation again and state if the following statements are vrai or faux:**

a Room 43 is on the third floor.

b Room 43 is equipped with two beds.

c The Wilsons want their breakfast at half past eight.

d Their suitcases are heavy.

e The lift is at the end of the corridor on the left.

5 You found a central hotel in the 5th district on the Internet. Judging from its description, it seems quiet and comfortable, which is just what you are looking for.

Hôtel Relais
St Jacques

****

3, rue de l'Abbé de l'épée, 75005 Paris
Métro St Michel (4)
Luxembourg (RER B)
Tél: 33 (0) 1 43 40 77 79

Proche du jardin du Luxembourg, sur une petite place calme, cet hôtel de pur style Haussmannien offre à ses visiteurs luxe, confort, modernité et spiritualité.

You make your way there to book a room for two. Follow the prompts to take part in the conversation.

Vous	*Say 'good evening' and ask if they have a room.*
Réceptionniste	Oui, qu'est-ce que vous voulez comme chambre? Une chambre pour une personne?
Vous	*Say 'no, a double room with two beds and a bathroom'.*
Réceptionniste	C'est pour combien de nuits?
Vous	*It's for four nights.*
Réceptionniste	Oui, j'ai une chambre avec salle de bains.
Vous	*How much is it?*
Réceptionniste	Alors, pour quatre nuits, nous faisons une promotion.
Vous	*Ask what 'promotion' is.*
Réceptionniste	Une promotion? C'est une offre spéciale. Vous restez chez nous quatre nuits, mais vous ne payez que trois nuits. Donc 140€ par nuit multipliés par trois, ça vous fait un total de 420€ au lieu de 560€.
Vous	*Ask if breakfast is included.*
Réceptionniste	Oui, le petit déjeuner est compris.
Vous	*Ask what time breakfast is served.*
Réceptionniste	Entre huit heures et dix heures.
Vous	*Ask if you can have a meal in the hotel.*
Réceptionniste	Mais oui, bien sûr. Le restaurant est au premier étage.
Vous	*Ask who Haussmann is.*
Réceptionniste	Le Baron Haussmann a modernisé Paris au 19ème siècle. C'est lui qui a créé les grandes avenues.

12.05 **Now listen to the audio to confirm your answers.**

Go further

SE PLAINDRE *COMPLAINING*

Things aren't always as they ought to be and you may have to complain about things not working (… **ne marche(nt) pas**) or things that are missing (**il n'y a pas de…**). If the situation is really bad you can always ask to speak to the **gérant** (*manager*).

6 Use the words in the box to complain to the gérant. Explain which objects (in the square boxes) are not working and which (in the circles) are missing.

l'eau chaude	le savon	les couvertures
	la douche	
le radiateur	la lampe	les serviettes	la télévision

L'ALPHABET FRANÇAIS *THE FRENCH ALPHABET*

Knowing the French alphabet is very useful. You may be asked to spell your name when booking accommodation or tickets (**Ça s'écrit comment?** or **Vous pouvez épeler?**).

7 Read the alphabet below several times and practise spelling your name and your address.

A	B	C	D	E	F	G
ah	bé	cé	dé	eux	eff	j'ai
H	I	J	K	L	M	N
ahsh	ee	j'y	kah	elle	emm	enne
O	P	Q	R	S	T	U
oh	pé	ku	erre	ess	té	u*
V	W	X	Y	Z		
vé	doubl'vé	eeks	ee grec	zed		

*as in **du**

RÉSERVER EN LIGNE, ENVOYER UN COURRIEL *BOOKING ONLINE, SENDING AN EMAIL*

Si vous avez l'intention de réserver un hôtel en France, **il vaut mieux** (*it's better*) réserver longtemps à l'avance surtout pendant les périodes de vacances. Lorsque la réservation est faite en ligne il est généralement demandé de payer une **caution** (*a safety deposit*) pour garantir la réservation.

8 John wrote un courriel (*an email*) to the owner of a **gîte rural** (*a self-catering cottage*) in which he asked several questions. Read the reply John received, and answer the questions.

a Has his reservation been accepted? Is it fully guaranteed?

To: josborne@hotmail.com
Subject: Réservation gîte rural

Cher Monsieur Osborne

J'ai le plaisir de confirmer votre réservation dans notre gîte du 15 au 22 août.

Je réponds à vos questions:

a Entre quatre et six personnes peuvent dormir confortablement dans le gîte.

b Non, il n'y a pas besoin d'amener des draps et des serviettes car nous les fournissons.

c Oui, nous acceptons les chiens.

d Je vous demande une caution de 200€ par carte bancaire pour garantir votre réservation.

À très bientôt le plaisir de vous voir.

Jacques Proment, propriétaire du gîte Les Cyprès

Now write in French the four questions John is likely to have asked in his email.

    b Nous sommes une famille avec quatre enfants, combien _____?

    c Est-ce qu'il faut _____?

    d _____?

    e Qu'est-ce qu'il faut _____?

Go further

There are many websites you can use to learn more about accommodation in France, and to book your next holiday, of course. The more reliable ones are sponsored by **les offices du tourisme** (*official tourism boards*) and **les syndicats d'initiative** (*local associations*):

▶ Maison de la France: www.franceguide.com
▶ L'office du tourisme à Paris: www.paris-touristoffice.com
▶ FNOTSI (Fédération Nationale des Offices de Tourisme et Syndicats d'Initiative): www.tourisme.fr

Pour louer des logements touristiques:

▶ Syndicat National des Résidences de Tourisme: www.snrt.fr
▶ CléVacances: www.clevacances.com/FR

9 **You've been browsing an airline magazine and stumbled upon an advert for rural accommodation in Normandy. Read it and answer the questions.**

PROMOTIONS EN NORMANDIE

SEINE-MARITIME : -10% sur vos vacances d'été

Profitez d'une réduction de 10% sur le tarif de location semaine jusqu'au 1er septembre: un break à prix réduit pour vos vacances en Normandie.

Nous vous proposons une grande sélection de logements en ville et à la campagne. Nos gîtes ruraux sont parfaitement équipés en cuisine et linge de maison. Nos chambres d'hôtes sont disponibles en demi-pension ou en pension complète.

---

réduction	*discount*
tarif de location	*rental fees*
gîtes ruraux	*plural of* **gîte rural**
linge de maison	*linen*

a Which two kinds of accommodation are available?
b How long is the offer running?
c What kind of equipment is provided with every rental unit?

? Test yourself

1 Can you find the missing words to complete these sentences?

   a Je cherche un hôtel deux _____. Je n'aime pas le grand luxe.

   b Je voudrais _____ une chambre pour trois nuits, s'il vous plaît.

   c Il y a un petit problème: la douche ne _____ pas.

   d Est-ce qu'il faut payer une _____ pour garantir la réservation?

   e Prenez l'_____ en face de la réception. Le restaurant est au troisième étage.

2 What questions would you ask to get these answers?

   a Oui, nous avons des chambres de libre.

   b Je suis désolé, les animaux ne sont pas acceptés dans l'hôtel.

   c C'est 145€ par nuit pour deux personnes.

   d Ah, non. Pour l'internet, c'est 3€15 en plus.

   e Bien sûr, vous pouvez prendre le petit déjeuner dans votre chambre.

SELF CHECK

	I CAN...
○	. . . ask for information at the tourist office.
○	. . . practise booking into a hotel.
○	. . . complain about things missing/not working.
○	. . . spell my name.
○	. . . book accommodation online.

13

Bien manger, bien boire

Eating and drinking well

In this unit you will learn how to:
▶ *recognize some typical French dishes.*
▶ *practise ordering a snack.*
▶ *choose a menu and order a meal.*

Before you start, revise:
▶ *saying what you want (Unit 7, Section 2).*
▶ *the verb **prendre** (Unit 5, Section 7).*
▶ *some, any (Unit 2, Section 3).*
▶ *asking questions (Unit 5, Section 1).*
▶ *likes and dislikes (Unit 8, Section 2).*

📷 Manger au restaurant

La cuisine en France est très variée; chaque région offre ses produits et spécialités gastronomiques. Grâce à sa population importante d'immigrés, la France a une cuisine ethnique riche et relativement bon marché. Par contre, les restaurants végétariens sont rares.

On mange très bien dans des restaurants modestes appelés les petits restaurants du coin. Au menu ils ont souvent des **plats** (*dishes*) simples mais appétissants comme un pâté maison et un **plat garni** (*main course with a side*). On peut aussi manger dans une brasserie et commander un plat unique où on choisira entre un **bifteck-frites** (*steak with chips*), une excellente spécialité, et le **plat du jour** (*daily special*).

Le **pourboire** (*tip*) est toujours inclus dans **l'addition** (*bill*). Si vous êtes satisfait, vous pouvez laisser quelques euros pour le **serveur** ou la **serveuse** (*waiter*).

La **restauration rapide** (*fast food*) à la française est une autre option: on peut manger pour pas cher dans une crêperie, ou au 'macdo' (McDonald's pour les Français) par exemple.

Les restaurants proposent en général plusieurs menus (gastronomique, touristique) et la carte.

1 Can you match the restaurant type to its definition?

a	une brasserie	**1**	a fast food place
b	un restaurant gastronomique	**2**	a cross between a café and a restaurant
c	une crêperie	**3**	a gourmet restaurant
d	un resto rapide	**4**	a pancake house

2 Without looking back at the reading, choose the correct phrase to complete the following statements.

a Fast-food can easily/cannot be found.

b **Les petits restaurants du coin** usually serve simple/ethnic food.

c **Un plat garni** is a dish with meat only/meat and a side of vegetables.

d In a **brasserie** one can eat pancakes/a limited range of dishes.

e **Le plat du jour** is the daily special/a dish with cold food.

f **Crêperies** serve pancakes/a full breakfast menu.

Vocabulary builder

13.01 Listen to the vocabulary and try to imitate the pronunciation of the native speakers.

POUR COMMANDER *ORDERING FOOD*

Qu'est-ce que c'est le/la/les...?	*What's the...?*
C'est quoi le/la/les...?	*What's the...?*
Je vais en prendre un/une.	*I'll take one*
Pour commencer...	*To start with...*
comme entrée	*as a starter*
comme plat principal	*as a main course*
comme dessert	*for dessert*
saignant/à point/bien cuit	*rare/medium/well done*
ensuite	*then*

How would you tell a waiter that you'd like your bifteck (*steak*) well done?

Je voudrais _____ .

BOISSONS ET SNACKS *DRINKS AND SNACKS*

de la bière en bouteille	*bottled beer*
une bière pression	*draught beer*
un café	*a black coffee*
un café crème	*a white coffee (with milk not cream)*
un thé au citron	*lemon tea*
un thé nature	*tea (without milk, etc...)*
un thé avec du lait froid	*tea with cold milk*
une orange pressée	*freshly squeezed orange*
un jus de fruit	*fruit juice*
un jus de pomme/d'ananas/de pamplemousse	*apple/pineapple/grapefruit juice*
des sandwiches au jambon et au fromage	*ham and cheese sandwiches*
une glace à la vanille	*vanilla ice cream*

How would you ask a waiter if they have pineapple juice?

POUR PARLER AU SERVEUR *TALKING WITH THE WAITER*

Qu'est-ce que vous avez...	*What do you have...*
...à manger?	*...to eat?*
...à boire?	*...to drink?*
Qu'est-ce que vous avez...	*What do you have in the way...*
...comme boissons/snacks?	*...of drinks/snacks?*
...comme parfums?	*...of flavours?*
Vous désirez?	*What will you have?*
Vous avez choisi?	*Have you made a choice?*
Il n'y a plus de pain.	*There is no more bread.*
Il ne reste plus de pain.	*There is no bread left.*

Conversation

À la terrasse d'un café deux touristes sont prêts à commander.

Two tourists sitting outside a café are ready to order. The man asks the waiter what a croque-monsieur is.

🎧 **3** 13.02 **Listen to the waiter's explanations, then answer the questions.**

Garçon	Bonjour, messieurs-dames. Qu'est-ce que vous désirez?
Homme	Qu'est-ce que vous avez à manger?
Garçon	À manger, nous avons des sandwiches au jambon blanc, rillettes, pâté de campagne, saucisson sec, hot-dogs, omelettes, croque-monsieur...
Homme	Qu'est-ce que c'est un croque-monsieur?
Garçon	Un croque-monsieur? C'est deux tranches de pain grillé avec jambon et fromage au milieu.
Homme	Ça a l'air délicieux ... je vais en prendre un.
Garçon	Et pour vous madame?
Femme	Moi, je crois que je vais prendre une omelette ... qu'est-ce que vous avez comme omelettes?
Garçon	Omelettes au fromage, aux champignons, aux herbes...
Femme	Une omelette aux champignons.
Garçon	Et comme boissons, Messieurs-dames?
Homme	Vous avez de la bière?
Garçon	Oui ... nous avons de la bière pression et de la Kronenbourg en bouteille.
Homme	Bon, une pression s'il vous plaît.
Garçon	Je vous sers un demi?
Homme	Oui, c'est ça.
Femme	Moi, je vais prendre un café crème.
Garçon	Bon, alors une pression, un café crème, une omelette aux champignons et un croque-monsieur.
Homme	Merci bien, monsieur.

rillettes	*type of potted meat, usually pork, similar to pâté*
tranche de pain grillé	*slice of toasted bread*
au milieu	*in the middle*
ça a l'air	*it seems*
les champignons	*mushrooms*
un demi	*half (usually half a pint, but sometimes half a litre)*

a How would you explain to someone English what a **croque-monsieur** is?

b What is the woman ordering?

c What expression does the woman use to mean *I think I'll have...*?

d What drinks are they having?

4 **See if you can unscramble the dialogue below, starting with 1.**

_____ **a** Je vais prendre une pression.

_____ **b** À manger nous avons des sandwiches, des croque-monsieur, des pizzas...

___1___ **c** Bonjour Monsieur, qu'est-ce que vous désirez?

_____ **d** De la pression et de la Kronenbourg en bouteille.

_____ **e** Qu'est-ce que vous avez à manger?

_____ **f** Je vais prendre une pizza; et comme bières, qu'est-ce que vous avez?

5 **You're hungry and decide to go to a café for a snack. Here comes the waiter ... Follow the prompts to place your order.**

Serveuse	Qu'est-ce que vous désirez?
Vous	*Say that you would like a croque-monsieur.*
Serveuse	Je suis désolé, monsieur, mais il n'y a plus de jambon.
Vous	*Ask him if he has any omelettes.*
Serveuse	Alors, comme omelettes nous avons l'omelette nature, au jambon et l'omelette Parmentier.
Vous	*Ask what Parmentier is.*
Serveuse	L'omelette Parmentier? C'est une omelette avec des pommes de terre.
Vous	*Say that you'll take the potato omelette.*
Serveuse	Bien, alors une omelette Parmentier; et à boire, qu'est-ce que je vous sers?
Vous	*Ask him what he has in the way of fruit juice.*
Serveuse	Comme jus de fruit nous avons du jus d'orange, du jus d'ananas, du jus de pamplemousse...
Vous	*Say that you will have a pineapple juice and the bill, please.*
Serveuse	Oui bien sûr, tout de suite.

13.03 **Now listen to the dialogue and check you answers.**

6 Using the menu and the previous activity as a guide, act out similar situations varying the dishes and drinks.

BRASSERIE LUTÉCIA

Salades composées

Salade mixte 10,00
Tomates, salade, œuf

Salade végétarienne 10,80
Tomates, poivron, maïs,
carotte, concombre,
salade

Chef salade 11,00
Tomates, pommes à
l'huile, jambon, gruyère,
salade, œuf dur

Salade niçoise 13,00
Tomates, œuf, thon,
poivrons, concombre,
olives, salade, anchois

Buffet chaud

Croque monsieur 7,00

Croque madame 7,50

Omelette nature
(3 pièces) 7,50
Omelette jambon 8,50
Omelette fromage 8,50

Buffet froid

Poulet froid
mayonnaise 11,50
Assiette charcuterie 11,30
Assiette de viande froide   11,30

Sandwiches

Pâté ou rillettes 5,00
Camembert ou Gruyère .. 5,00
Saucisson sec ou à l'ail 5,00

Boissons

Café express 3,60

Thé au citron 4,60

Jus de fruit 4,60

Bière pression 4,60

Bière bouteille 4,60

Eau minérale 3,60

Soda 3,60

Apéritif anisé 7,00

Conversation

A tourist finds an authentically Art Deco bistro in the centre of Paris. He likes the menu and decides to try it out.

Menu à 33€
En entrée
L'œuf cocotte au foie gras,
La soupe gratinée à l'oignon,
Le Crottin de chèvre chaud et salade

En plat
Le confit de canard
La poule au pot d'Henry IV garnie maison
Le steak au poivre avec sa garniture

Dessert
La crème brûlée à l'ancienne
Les profiteroles au chocolat
La tarte des demoiselles Tatin à la crème

7 13.04 **Read the menu, and then listen to the first part of the conversation between the tourist and the waiter:**

Tourist	Vous avez une table pour une personne?
Serveur	Oui, monsieur, il nous en reste juste une près de la fenêtre.
Later...	Alors, qu'est-ce que ce sera pour vous, le menu à 33€ ou la carte?
Tourist	Je vais prendre le menu.
Serveur	Qu'est-ce que je vous sers comme entrée?
Tourist	Je crois que je préfère la soupe à l'oignon.
Serveur	Une soupe gratinée, alors. Bien et ensuite?
Tourist	Le steak au poivre.
Serveur	Vous le voulez comment? Saignant, à point ou bien cuit?
Tourist	À point. Vous le servez avec quoi le steak?
Serveur	Avec une garniture de légumes de saison, haricots verts, carottes et une salade verte. Vous prendrez quelque chose à boire?
Tourist	Oui, de l'eau minérale et puis une bouteille de Bordeaux. Vous pouvez me conseiller pour le vin?
Serveur	Oui, d'accord, je vous apporte un bon Bordeaux.

Answer these questions:

a What formula does the tourist choose, a set menu or la carte?

b What does he have for his starter?

c Is the pepper steak a **plat garni**? How can you tell?

d How does he want his steak cooked?

13.05 **Now listen to the end of the conversation.**

Serveur	C'était bon?
Tourist	Très bon, merci.
Serveur	Vous avez choisi un dessert?
Tourist	Comme dessert, je vais prendre la tarte des demoiselles Tatin à la crème.
Serveur	Je vous la recommande ... elle est délicieuse et faite maison. Vous prendrez bien un café après la tarte?
Tourist	Non merci, et amenez l'addition après le dessert, s'il vous plaît.

C'était bon?	Did you enjoy your meal (lit. Was it good?)

8 13.06 **Now listen to the complete dialogue and spot the French version of the following phrases:**

a Is there a table for one?

b I think that I prefer...

c How would you like it (the steak)?

d Can you advise me about the wine?

f Have you chosen a dessert?

g Bring the bill after dessert.

9 **Now it's your turn. Follow the prompts and order a meal.**

Serveuse	Bonjour, monsieur/madame, vous avez choisi?
You	*Say that to start with you'll have a filet de hareng.*
Serveuse	Je regrette, il n'y a plus de filet de hareng.
You	*Say that you'll have an avocat à la vinaigrette.*
Serveuse	Bien, un avocat a la vinaigrette, et ensuite ...
You	*Ask what is cassoulet.*
Serveuse	C'est une spécialité française avec de la viande de porc et haricots blancs.
You	*Say that you don't like beans. Say you prefer the grillade du jour with frites.*
Serveuse	Vous la voulez comment, votre viande?
You	*Say medium and say that you would also like a bottle of sauvignon.*

After the starter...

Serveuse	Voilà. Une grillade avec des frites.
You	*Ask what she has in the way of desserts.*
Serveuse	Fromage, glaces, crème au caramel.
You	*Say that you'll have a vanilla ice cream.*
Serveuse	Ah, je regrette mais nous n'avons plus de vanille.
You	*Ask what other flavours they have.*
Serveuse	Citron, café, chocolat, fraise.
You	*Say that you will have a strawberry ice cream.*

13.07 **Now listen to the conversation and check your answers. As you do, remember that there are possible variations in how the same questions can be asked.**

?? Test yourself

1 Say the following in French:

a What have you got in the way of snacks?

_____

b We prefer bottled beer.

_____

c I would like an apple juice, please.

_____

d Have you chose a starter? (formal)

_____

e I like my meat well done.

_____

f Can you bring me the bill, please?

_____

g There is no ham left.

_____

h What ice cream flavours do you have?

_____

2 In each line there is a word that does not belong. Can you spot it?

a citron, fraise, pamplemousse, pomme, glace
b bière, omelette, eau minérale, café crème, thé au lait
c boulangerie, brasserie, crêperie, hôtel-restaurant, bar
d champignons, haricots, cassoulet, avocat, carotte

SELF CHECK

I CAN...
⚪ . . . recognize some typical French dishes.
⚪ . . . practise ordering a snack.
⚪ . . . choose a menu and order a meal.

14 Les transports publics
Public transport

In this unit you will learn how to:
▶ *get on public transport in France.*
▶ *use appropriate expressions to travel
  by bus, taxi, train and underground.*
▶ *ask for specific travel information.*

Before you start, revise:
▶ *finding out what's available
  (Unit 2, Section 3).*
▶ *asking for and understanding directions (Unit 6, Section 1).*
▶ *expressions of time, days of the week (Unit 5, Vocabulary
  builder).*
▶ *numbers (Units 2–6).*

Getting round Paris

Le métro parisien est très pratique et économique. Le **réseau** (*network*) a 14 lignes identifiables par leur numéro et leurs directions (les deux stations terminus). Pour changer d'une ligne à l'autre, suivez les panneaux oranges qui indiquent la **correspondance** (*connection*) avec la ligne que vous désirez prendre. Le métro est joint au RER, qui dessert Paris et sa banlieue.

Avec un seul ticket (1€70), vous pouvez aller **n'importe où** (*anywhere*) dans Paris pendant deux heures. Le **tarif** (*rate*) est 25% moins cher quand on achète un **carnet** (*a set of 10 tickets*).

Mais pourquoi payer **plein tarif** (*full fare*)? Pour découvrir Paris et ses environs, achetez 'Paris Visite', un **forfait transport** (*travel pass*) qui inclue métro, tramway, bus, RER et trains SNCF. Ce forfait permet également de bénéficier de réductions sur l'entrée de nombreux sites touristiques de la capitale. **Il n'y a pas de meilleure façon** (*there's no better way*) de connaître Paris.

What two ways of saving on the full fare price in the Paris metro are mentioned in the text?

Vocabulary builder

14.01

PAR LE RAIL *BY RAIL*

le billet/ticket	*ticket (train/underground/bus)*
le trajet, le voyage	*travel, journey*
le métro/le RER (réseau express régional)	*the underground/express suburban link*
la gare	*(train) station*
le guichet	*ticket office*
une place	*a seat (also square – la place du Marché)*
un aller (simple)	*single ticket*
un aller-retour	*return ticket*
un horaire	*timetable*
le prochain/dernier train	*the next/last train*
À quelle heure part/arrive le train?	*What time does the train leave/arrive?*

PAR LA ROUTE *BY ROAD*

la station de taxis	*taxi rank*
l'autobus (m) (bus)	*town bus*
l'autocar (m) (car)	*coach/long distance bus*
la gare routière	*bus station*
l'autocar quitte Paris à quelle heure ?	*What time deos the coach leave Paris?*

Complete the sentences with words from the Vocabulary builder.

   a Sur le réseau parisien, le _____ est joint avec le RER.
   b Il faut prendre l'autocar à la _____.
   c Un _____ est toujours plus économique qu'un aller simple.
   d Pour savoir quand les trains partent, il faut consulter l'_____.
   e Allez au _____ pour acheter votre billet.
   f Le _____ entre Paris et Nantes prend combien de temps?
   g Il y a une grosse différence de prix entre un ticket de métro et un
      _____ de train.

NEW EXPRESSIONS

C'est quelle direction?	*Which line (lit. 'direction') is it?*
Où est-ce que je peux...?	*Where can I...?*
Où est-ce qu'il faut...?	*Where do you have to...?*
Vous devez changer.	*You must change.*
C'est quelle ligne?	*What number (bus) is it?*
jusqu'au bout de la ligne	*till the end of the line*
arriver, quitter	*arrive, leave*
voyager de jour, de nuit	*travel in the daytime, overnight*
dans la matinée, soirée	*in the morning, evening*
manquer la sortie	*miss the exit*

Practice

1 How would you ask the following questions in French?

   a Where do I have to take the bus?

   b I would like to travel in the morning.

   c Must I change underground lines?

   d What RER line goes to Charles de Gaulle airport?

2 14.02 *A traveller stops at **le bureau de renseignements** (information office) and asks how to get to the Gare du Nord from Orly-Sud. He has trouble following the directions he's given.*

Listen to the conversation and answer the questions.

   a Which two expressions are hints that he doesn't understand what he's being told?

Can you do better than him? Listen again and indicate if the following statements are vrai ou faux. You can look at the diagram in the next activity to check the place names.

   b Il faut prendre la liaison (*underground link*) jusqu'à Orlyval Anthony.

   c Ensuite, il faut prendre la ligne C du RER.

   d Pour aller à l'aéroport, le bus est plus rapide.

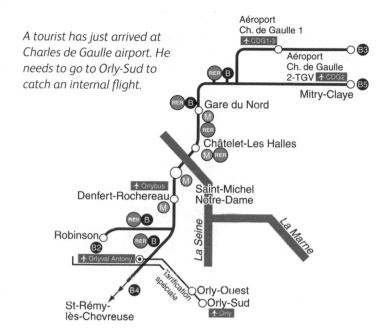

A tourist has just arrived at Charles de Gaulle airport. He needs to go to Orly-Sud to catch an internal flight.

3 Look at the diagram then complete the dialogue with the words from the box.

manquerez   mener (*take to*)   changer   prenez   direction

Touriste	Pardon Monsieur c'est quelle **(a)** _____ pour l'Aeroport Orly-Sud?
Homme	Orly? Vous **(b)** _____ la ligne B du RER direction St-Rémy-lès-Chevreuse.
Touriste	C'est direct?
Homme	Non, il faut **(c)** _____ à la station Antony.
Touriste	Bon, je dois changer à Antony et puis?
Homme	Là, vous avez la liaison Orlyval. C'est un métro automatique qui va vous **(d)** _____ aux aéroports d'Orly.
Touriste	C'est pas compliqué.
Homme	Non, mais faites bien attention de prendre direction B4 St-Rémy-lès-Chevreuse. Si vous prenez la direction B2, vous **(e)** _____ la station d'Antony.
Touriste	Ah, merci, Monsieur.

LA STATION DE TAXIS *THE TAXI RANK*

 4 14.03 **Listen carefully to the conversation and answer the questions.**

    a The tourist doesn't get any information from the first passer-by: why?

Touriste	Pardon, Monsieur, où est la station de taxis la plus proche?
Homme	Je ne sais pas, je ne suis pas d'ici…
Later…	
Touriste	S'il vous plaît, Madame, savez-vous où il y a une station de taxis?
Femme	Mais oui, c'est très simple, vous en avez une, à 500 mètres, à côté de la Gare du Nord.
Touriste	La Gare du Nord, c'est où exactement?
Femme	Bon, il faut d'abord monter le boulevard Magenta. Au carrefour, vous allez continuer tout droit et prendre le boulevard Denain et à droite de la Gare du Nord vous allez trouver la station de taxis.

    b How far is the taxi rank?

    c At the crossroads does he have to go right or straight on?

5 Would you be able to find the taxi rank? Choose the correct word:

    a Il faut monter means:

        1 turn   **2** go up   **3** cross

    b Un carrefour means:

        1 crossroads   **2** traffic lights   **3** sign post

    c Vous continuez tout droit means:

        1 turn left   **2** turn right   **3** carry straight on

VOYAGER EN AUTOBUS *TRAVELLING BY BUS*

6 **Read the following passage about how the metro and bus tickets work in Paris. Fill in the missing words with the ones from the box.**

magasins   ligne   acheter   carnets   tickets

À Paris, on utilise les mêmes tickets pour le métro et pour l'autobus. On peut (**a**) _____ un ticket simple dans l'autobus, mais avec un carnet de tickets, c'est plus économique. Les (**b**) _____ sont vendus dans certaines stations de métro ou d'autobus. Ils se trouvent aussi dans certains (**c**) _____ de livres (FNAC) ou de tabac. Avec un ticket d'autobus vous pouvez aller jusqu'au bout de la (**d**) _____ . Avec deux (**e**) _____ , vous pouvez aller n'importe où dans la ville de Paris.

À LA GARE ROUTIÈRE *AT THE BUS STATION*

7 14.04 **A tourist is finding out about buses and tickets. What is she advised to do?**

Touriste	Pardon, Monsieur, c'est quelle ligne pour aller à la Gare d'Austerlitz?
Homme	Alors pour la Gare d'Austerlitz le plus simple c'est de prendre la ligne 57...
Touriste	C'est direct?
Homme	Non, il faut changer au deuxième arrêt, puis vous prenez la ligne 24.
Touriste	C'est loin à pied?
Homme	D'ici? Ah oui, vous ne pouvez pas y aller à pied.
Touriste	Le prochain bus part à quelle heure?
Homme	Dans dix minutes.
Touriste	Et ... où est-ce que je peux acheter un ticket?
Homme	Au guichet là-bas...
Later...	
Touriste	Je voudrais acheter un ticket aller-retour pour la Gare d'Austerlitz.
Femme	Il n'y a pas de tickets aller-retour. Achetez deux tickets ou bien alors un carnet, c'est plus pratique et moins cher.
Touriste	Un carnet, qu'est-ce que c'est?
Femme	C'est dix tickets pour le prix de sept.
Touriste	Très bien. Je vais prendre un carnet.

ÊTRE DANS LE BON AUTOBUS *ON THE RIGHT BUS*

8 14.05 **The same tourist asks the driver where she should get off. Can you understand where?**

Touriste	Ce bus va bien à la Gare d'Austerlitz?
Chauffeur	Oui, c'est bien ça.
Touriste	Vous pouvez me dire où il faut descendre?
Chauffeur	Oui, bien sûr. C'est très facile. C'est le premier arrêt une fois que vous avez traversé la Seine.
Touriste	Euh ... oui mais je ne connais pas Paris. Il faut combien de temps pour arriver à la gare?
Chauffeur	Oh, une bonne demi-heure. Dans trente minutes vous allez passer sur le pont et juste après vous descendrez.

9 How would you say the following?

a What bus number goes to the Gare d'Austerlitz?

b Is it direct?

c Is it far on foot?

d At what time does the next bus leave?

e Where can I buy a ticket?

f I would like to buy a return ticket to les Invalides.

g I'll take a set of tickets.

h How long does it take to get to the station?

AU BUREAU DE RENSEIGNEMENTS *AT THE INFORMATION OFFICE*

10 14.06 **At la Gare de Lyon in Paris, a man enquires about trains. Listen to the conversation, then answer the questions.**

a Where does the man want to go?

Homme	Bonjour, Madame, je voudrais un aller pour Marseille.
Hôtesse	Marseille ... bon. Vous voyagez quel jour?
Homme	Le 10 juin ... un samedi.
Hôtesse	À quelle heure voulez-vous quitter Paris?
Homme	Dans la matinée.
Hôtesse	Bon, vous avez quatre TGV: le premier part à 8.20, le deuxième à 9.20, le troisième à 10.20, le quatrième à 11.20.
Homme	Celui de 10.20 me convient très bien.
Hôtesse	Il quitte Paris Gare de Lyon à 10.20 et arrive à Marseille St Charles à 13.29. La réservation est obligatoire.
Homme	D'accord, bon alors, il met un peu plus de trois heures?
Hotesse	Oui, c'est bien ça.
Homme	C'est combien l'aller simple?
Hôtesse	Vous avez une réduction?
Homme	Non, je n'ai pas de carte.
Hôtesse	OK, alors en 1ère ou en 2ème classe?
Homme	En 2ème classe.
Hôtesse	Alors en seconde classe, l'aller tarif normal coûte 94€, la réservation est incluse dans le prix.
Homme	Oh, c'est un peu cher. Il y a moins cher?
Hôtesse	Le train qui quitte Paris à 9.20 est moins cher. C'est un billet «Découverte Séjour» et l'aller coûte 57€60. Ça vous va?
Homme	Oui, c'est beaucoup mieux.
Hôtesse	Vous avez le choix entre un siège côté fenêtre ou côté couloir.
Homme	Je préfère côté fenêtre.

b Which train does he want to catch?

c Where does he want to sit?

celui de ... me convient	*the one at ... suits me*
il met un peu plus de...	*it takes a bit more than...*
beaucoup mieux	*much better*

Have you noticed what the French say for *on the train*? How would you say *I'm on the train*?

11 Before taking the part of the traveller in this conversation, look at the Marseille–Paris train timetable from the **SNCF (Societé Nationale des Chemins de Fer).**

MARSEILLE St CHARLES–PARIS						
Départ à	12h12	12h27	13h29	14h31	15h29	19h29
Meilleur prix	77.20€	94.00€	94.00€	94.00€	94.00€	38.90€
Durée	10h37	03h14	03h12	03h00	03h16	03h12

Vous	*Ask for a return to Paris on the 8th October in the afternoon.*
Employé	Alors vous avez plusieurs trains qui quittent Marseille St Charles l'après-midi. Il y a un train toutes les heures.
Vous	*Ask how long the journey lasts.*
Employé	Environ trois heures, trois heures et quart.
Vous	*Say that you do not want to arrive in Paris after 19.00.*
Employé	Alors dans ce cas vous pouvez prendre le train qui quitte St Charles à 13.29, ou à 14.31 ou même à 15.29.
Vous	*Say that the 15.29 train suits you and ask for the price of the ticket in second class.*
Employé	Le billet en 2ème classe tarif plein coûte 94€.
Vous	*Say that it is a little expensive. Ask if there is something cheaper.*
Employé	Alors, un instant ... Le train de 12.12 est moins cher. Le prix du billet aller-retour ne coûte que 77€20.
Vous	*Ask at what time the train arrives in Paris.*
Employé	Le train met 10.37 pour arriver à Paris.
Vous	*Say that it is too long and that you will take the 15.20 train.*
Employé	D'accord...

There are several ways of asking in French how long the journey takes. The third form using il faut is probably the easiest way:

Le trajet dure (*lasts*) combien de temps?
Le train/bus/taxi met (lit. *puts*) combien de temps?
Il faut combien de temps pour le trajet/le voyage?

Test yourself

1 Complete the sentences with the missing words.

a Ce n'est pas une ligne directe. Il faut prendre une _____ à La Chapelle.

b Je préfère un siège _____ couloir.

c Avec une carte de _____, on paie le billet de train moins cher.

d Pour arriver à quinze heures, il faut partir dans la _____.

e Pour visiter Notre Dame, prenez la ligne 4 et _____ à St Michel.

2 Do you remember the French for the following?

a I would like a set of tickets.

_____

b I would like a return ticket to Grenoble.

_____

c Which direction is it for the Gare Austerlitz?

_____

d The next bus leaves at what time?

_____

e Where can I buy a ticket?

_____

f How long does the journey take?

_____

g Do I need/is it necessary for me to book a seat?

_____

SELF CHECK

I CAN...
...get on public transport in France.
...use appropriate expressions to travel by bus, taxi, train and underground.
...ask for specific travel information.

15 Faire du tourisme
Sightseeing

In this unit you will learn how to:
▶ *ask for a town map.*
▶ *find out about visiting places of interest.*
▶ *practise buying admission tickets.*
▶ *plan a visit to French museums.*
▶ *book an excursion.*

Before you start, revise:
▶ *saying what you want (Unit 7, Section 2).*
▶ *asking for and understanding directions (Unit 6, Section 1).*
▶ *expressions of time, days of the week (Unit 5, Vocabulary builder).*

Planning a visit

Dès votre arrivée dans une ville ou une région, rendez-vous à l'office de tourisme le plus proche pour demander un **plan** (*a map*) ainsi que des brochures sur la ville et ses **environs** (*surroundings*). Le personnel peut répondre à toutes vos questions et vous donner des **renseignements** (*information*) utiles sur les visites, musées, loisirs, **manifestations culturelles** (*cultural events*). Si vous désirez mieux connaitre une région, renseignez-vous sur les **excursions** (*outings*) qui suivent (*follow*) des circuits touristiques. Les régions de France ont un riche **patrimoine** (*heritage*) et des circuits sont souvent organisés pour explorer l'histoire ou les industries locales, comme La Route des vins de Bourgogne.

En France, il y a de nombreux **jours fériés** (*bank holidays*). Il est prudent de les connaître parce que les magasins, **musées** (*museums*) et monuments historiques sont souvent fermés ces jours-là.

🎙 Vocabulary builder

15.01 Listen and try to imitate the pronunciation of the speakers.

RENSEIGNEMENTS TOURISTIQUES *TOURIST INFORMATION*

le plan de la ville	*town map*
Qu'est-ce qu'il y a à faire?	*What is there to do?*
Qu'est-ce qu'il y a à voir?	*What is there to see?*
Qu'est-ce qu'on peut visiter dans les environs?	*What is there to visit (lit. What can one visit) in the area?*
une visite guidee	*guided tour*
faire une promenade/balade	*to go for a walk*
à pied, à vélo, en voiture, en bateau	*on foot, on a bike, by car, by boat*
faire une excursion	*to go on an excursion*
pique-niquer	*to picnic*
l'aire de jeux	*children's playground*
l'entrée	*way in, admission charge*
le tarif réduit	*reduced rate*
le plein tarif	*full rate*
un justificatif	*proof (of age, occupation, etc.)*
en pleine saison	*in high season*
hors saison	*out of season*
accès (m) gratuit	*free entry*
nocturne	*late-night opening*
une agence de voyages	*travel agency*

Hide the vocabulary. Can you remember the opposite of plein tarif and en pleine saison?

How would you say: *We go for a bike ride on Sundays? Come for a walk with us.*

The expressions **faire une balade** and **faire une promenade** often refer to different kinds of outings: **une balade à vélo**, **une balade en bateau**, **une promenade en voiture**. When the means of transport is not specified, it always means *on foot*: **une promenade/balade en forêt** (*a walk in the forest*).

Conversation

À L'OFFICE DU TOURISME *AT THE TOURIST OFFICE*

🎧 **1** 15.02 **Listen to the recording, then answer the following questions.**

Touriste	Bonjour, Madame, je voudrais un plan de la ville, s'il vous plaît.
Hôtesse	Oui, voilà.
Touriste	Nous ne sommes pas d'ici. Qu'est-ce qu'il y a à voir à Orléans?
Hôtesse	Il y a beaucoup de monuments historiques, surtout dans la vieille ville, comme la maison de Jeanne d'Arc, au numéro 52 sur le plan, à côté de la cathédrale Sainte-Croix; et puis il y a une belle promenade à pied à faire le long de la Loire. Du pont George V, vous avez une vue magnifique sur la Loire.
Touriste	Et qu'est-ce qu'il y a à faire pour les enfants?
Hôtesse	Près d'ici, il y a une piscine couverte ou même le Musée des sciences naturelles qui se trouve rue Émile Zola. Un peu plus loin, vous avez le Parc Floral.
Touriste	Et pour aller au Parc Floral ... il y a un bus?
Hôtesse	Oui, vous avez un autobus toutes les 30 minutes. Il part du centre-ville, place du Martroi.

a Can you name at least three things the tourist could see or do?
b How would you ask for a town map?
c Ask what there is to see.
d Ask what there is to do for the children.
e Ask if there is an indoor swimming pool.
f Ask if there is a bus to go to the Parc Floral.

2 The names of some French public holidays are listed on the right. Match the dates with the corresponding holidays:

a	1 janvier	**1**	Toussaint
b	1er mai	**2**	Noël
c	8 mai	**3**	Fête de la Vierge
d	14 juillet	**4**	Jour de l'An
e	15 août	**5**	Fête du travail
f	1er novembre	**6**	Victoire 1945
g	11 novembre	**7**	Armistice 1918
h	25 décembre	**8**	Fête Nationale

> July 14 is the most celebrated public holiday in France. Every significant town puts on its own celebration with a public dance and fireworks, as well as military ceremonies, to mark the **fête nationale**. In Paris, **le Président de la République** always attends the traditional military parade which marches down the Champs Elysées at 10 a.m. and is broadcast to the nation.

LES MUSÉES *MUSEUMS*

3 Read the passage for general knowledge, then answer the questions.

Les musées et monuments sont généralement ouverts tous les jours, sauf le lundi ou le mardi, de 10 à 12h et de 14 à 18h en été. Ces horaires peuvent varier. La **plupart** sont fermés les jours fériés. L'**entrée** est généralement **gratuite** pour les moins de 18 ans. Les étudiants, **personnes âgées** et **enseignants** ont droit à une réduction (entre 30% et 50%) sur présentation d'un justificatif, et quelquefois l'entrée est gratuite un jour par semaine.

    a What expression is used to refer to children under 18?

    b Can you guess the meaning of the words and expressions in bold?

4 Complete the passage with the missing words from the box.

forfait   carte   offices   librement   monuments

Valable deux, quatre ou six jours, la (**a**) _____ musées-monuments permet
de visiter (**b**) _____ et sans attente 60 musées et monuments de Paris et
d'Île-de-France. Elle est en vente dans les musées et (**c**) _____, principales
stations de métro, (**d**) _____ de tourisme de Paris, magasins FNAC.
Le (**e**) _____ pour un jour est de 35€, pour quatre jours consécutifs 50€, et
six jours consécutifs: 65€.

> **CULTURE**
> FNAC is the largest French retailer of books, CDs and DVDs, computer software and
> hardware, television sets, cameras and video games.

**5 Look at the following information – this is the kind of
information you may find about places of interest – then answer
the questions:**

A

> **Art Moderne (Musée National d')**
> Centre Georges-Pompidou
> Place Georges Pompidou – 75004 Paris
> Tél. 01 44 78 12 33   Métro : Hôtel-de-ville, Rambuteau
>
> www.centrepompidou.fr   RER A : Châtelet-Les Halles
>
> *Ouvert tous les jours de 11h à 21h sauf mardi (avec possibilité de
> nocturnes pour les expositions). Plein tarif: 13€ – Tarif réduit: 11€.*
>
> *Ce billet est valable le jour même pour toutes les expositions en
> cours, le Musée et l'Atelier Brancusi.*
> *Accès gratuit le 1er dimanche de chaque mois.*
>
> Collection d'œuvres d'artistes modernes et d'artistes
> contemporains, sans oublier les architectes, les designers, les
> photographes ainsi que les cinéastes.

B

Cité des Sciences et de l'Industrie – la Villette
Centre Parc de la Villette
30, avenue Corentin-Cariou – 75019 Paris
Tél. 01 40 05 80 00   Métro: Porte-de-la-Villette
www.cite-sciences.fr

De 10h à 18h. Le dimanche de 10h à 19h. Fermé le lundi.
Plein tarif: 18€. Cité des enfants : 15€. Planétarium: 11€.
Tarif réduit : 17€ et 8€.

Située dans le parc de la Villette, la cité présente un panorama complet des sciences et techniques à travers des expositions, des spectacles, des maquettes, des conférences et des jeux interactifs.

C

Louvre (Musée du)
Entrée principale par la Pyramide
Cour Napoléon – 75001 Paris
Tél. 01 40 20 51 51   Métro : Palais-Royal-Musée-du-Louvre
www.louvre.fr

Ouvert tous les jours de 9h à 18h, sauf le mardi et certains jours fériés. Nocturnes les mercredis et vendredis jusqu'à 22h.
Plein tarif : 10€ – Tarif réduit : 6€ (de 18h à 21.45).
Gratuité appliquée aux jeunes de 18 à 25 ans (avec justificatif), enseignants en histoire, handicapés et le 1er dimanche de chaque mois.

Le Musée du Louvre, ancienne demeure des rois de France, et l'un des plus grands musées du monde.

D

> **Picasso (Musée National)**
> Hôtel Salé
> 5, rue de Thorigny – 75003 Paris
> Tél. 01 42 71 25 21
> Métro : Saint-Paul/Saint-Sébastien Froissart/Chemin Vert
> Bus: 29 – 96 – 69 – 75 www.musee-picasso.fr
> *Été: 9h30–18h – Hiver: 9h30–17h30.*
> *Nocturne le jeudi jusqu'à 20h. Plein tarif : 7€70. Tarif réduit*
> *(de 18 ans à 25 ans inclus) : 5€70*
> *Gratuit pour les moins de 18 ans et le premier dimanche de*
> *chaque mois.*
> *Fermé le mardi, le 1er janvier et le 25 décembre.*
>
> Installé dans l'Hôtel Salé (XVIIe siècle), le musée rassemble une
> importante collection des œuvres de l'artiste.

    a If you were in Paris on a Tuesday, what could you visit?
    b If you did not have much money, which day would you choose to
       visit the attractions above?
    c What could you visit late in the evening and when?
    d Which museum would most interest a child?

FAIRE UNE EXCURSION *GOING ON AN EXCURSION*

6 You're interested in French wines, so you've decided to go with
your partner on a coach excursion following **la route des vins de
Bourgogne**. Look at the information in the advertisement and
answer the questions:
    a At what time should you be at the bus stop in the morning?
    b How long do you stop at Vézelay?
    c Name at least two things you could do from lunchtime until 4 p.m.
    d How much is the excursion for two people?

7 **You and your friend decide to book the trip to Beaune. Speak for both of you.**

You	*Say you would like to go on the excursion of la route des vins de Bourgogne.*
Employé	Vous voulez réserver des places pour quel jour?
You	*Say you'd like two places for the 22nd July.*
Employé	Le 22 juillet? Bon ... ça va, il y a de la place ... ça fait 184€.
You	*Ask if the coach leaves from here.*
Employé	Non, le car part de la Place Denfert-Rochereau, devant le café de Belfort.
You	*Ask him to repeat.*
Employé	Oui, Place Denfert-Rochereau devant le café de Belfort; mais je vais vous donner tous ces renseignements par écrit.
You	*Thank him; ask what time the coach leaves.*
Employé	Le car part à 7.30 mais il faut être là à 7.15.
You	*Ask if you can buy some wine in the wine cellar.*
Employé	Oui, vous pouvez déguster et acheter des vins de Bourgogne à un prix spécial.

15.03 **Now listen to the dialogue and check your answers.**

8 15.04 Michel is discussing the possibility of going on a coach excursion to Versailles and Trianon with his friend Agnès. Read the questions first, so you know what to look and listen for. Then listen to the tour description.

a Jour de l'excursion choisi par Michel et Agnès?
b Heure du départ de Paris?
c Durée du tour?
d Programme de la visite?
e Prix de l'entrée de la visite?
f Qui paie pour l'excursion et pourquoi?

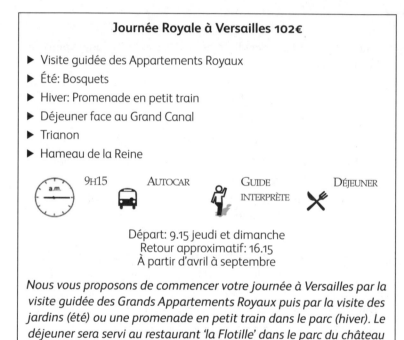

Journée Royale à Versailles 102€

▶ Visite guidée des Appartements Royaux
▶ Été: Bosquets
▶ Hiver: Promenade en petit train
▶ Déjeuner face au Grand Canal
▶ Trianon
▶ Hameau de la Reine

9h15   AUTOCAR   GUIDE   DÉJEUNER
                           INTERPRÈTE

Départ: 9.15 jeudi et dimanche
Retour approximatif: 16.15
À partir d'avril à septembre

Nous vous proposons de commencer votre journée à Versailles par la visite guidée des Grands Appartements Royaux puis par la visite des jardins (été) ou une promenade en petit train dans le parc (hiver). Le déjeuner sera servi au restaurant 'la Flotille' dans le parc du château en face du Grand Canal.

L'après-midi se poursuivra par la visite guidée des Trianon (vastes pavillons dans lesquels Louis XV et Louis XVI aimaient travailler et séjourner en retrait de la cour) et par la découverte du Hameau de la Reine Marie-Antoinette construit pour son divertissement.

Entrées incluses.

Test yourself

1 How would you say the following?

   a I would like a town map and information on the cathedral.

   b Is the park easy to find?

   c Does the museum shut between lunchtime and two?

   d One needs to be at the bus stop at what time?

2 Choose the appropriate word to complete this advert about guided tours of Paris.

> ### Découvrez Paris!
>
> En minibus, dans un autocar climatisé/loué ou en bateau/vélo sur la Seine.
>
> Formule rapide (3 heures) ou à la journée/semaine avec déjeuner inclus/guidé.
>
> Plusieurs choix de circuits à thème/promenade.
>
> Audio-guides bilingues fournis gratuitement/supplément.
>
> Programmes aussi organisés en hiver/soirée.

3 Unscramble the words to make questions.

   a a / ici ? / Qu'est-ce / y / faire / qu'il / à

   b musée / ouvert / Le / jours / est / les / fériés ?

   c gratuit / les / C'est / pour / de / dix-huit / moins / ans ?

   d faire / Tu / balade / viens/ une / à pied ?

   e La / de / visite / prend / combien / temps ?

SELF CHECK

	I CAN...
●	. . . ask for a town map.
●	. . . find out about visiting places of interest.
●	. . . practise buying admission tickets.
●	. . . plan a visit to French museums.
●	. . . book an excursion.

Sortir
Going out

In this unit you will learn how to:
▶ *find out what's on at night.*
▶ *book tickets for a concert.*
▶ *ask where you can play tennis and other sports.*

Before you start, revise:
▶ *finding out what's on and where (Unit 15, Vocabulary builder).*
▶ *saying precisely what you want (Unit 7, Section 2).*
▶ *talking about your likes and dislikes (Unit 8, Section 2).*
▶ *expressions of time, days of the week (Unit 5, Vocabulary builder).*

Looking for entertainment

Qu'est-ce qu'on peut faire pour se divertir? (*What can we do for entertainment?*) is the question most people ask themselves when they land in their holiday spot. And everyone has a different notion. Look for **une bonne ambiance** (*look for the right atmosphere*) with **un dîner aux chandelles** (*a candlelit dinner*) perhaps? Pick up a new sport by taking **des cours particuliers** (*private lessons*) avec **un moniteur** (*coach*)? Or simply spend a few **bonne soirées** (*good parties*) with new friends?

Pour les familles nombreuses (*large families*) free forms of entertainment like **faire une randonnée** (*go hiking*), or playing **un jeu de société** (*a board game*) quand il pleut, help to **profiter** (*enjoy/take advantage*) of the precious holiday time together.

What do you think the following words and expressions mean: **un divertissement, un moniteur de ski, un jeu de plage,** and **profiter du beau temps?**

Vocabulary builder

16.01 Listen to the new vocabulary and imitate the speakers.

LES DIVERTISSEMENTS *ENTERTAINMENT*

un spectacle	*a show*
une soirée	*evening entertainment, party*
un dîner-dansant	*dinner dance*
l'ambiance (f)	*atmosphere*
la salle	*room, hall, auditorium*
une restaurant boîte (de nuit)	*nightclub*
un piano-bar	*all-night restaurant with small band*
la place	*seat*
une séance	*performance, film showing*

FAIRE LE NÉCESSAIRE *MAKING ARRANGEMENTS*

louer	*to book, to hire*
la location	*hiring*
le bureau de location	*booking office*
prêter	*to lend*
le prêt	*lending*
entrée (f) libre/payante	*free admission/charge*
Il/Elle doit payer?	*He/She must pay?*
l'inscription (f)	*enrolment*
une carte d'abonnement	*season ticket*
un court de tennis	*tennis court*
un cours particulier	*private lesson*
faire du vélo	*to go cycling*

NEW EXPRESSIONS

Qu'est-ce qu'il y a comme...?	*What sort of ... is/are there?*
Qu'est-ce qu'on peut faire?	*What can I/we/one do?*
C'est combien l'heure?	*How much is it an hour?*
C'est combien la journée?	*How much is it a day?*
une veille de fêtes	*the day before public holidays*

Have you noticed the difference between the words cours and court? They are pronounced the same way, but what do they mean?

OÙ ALLER? *WHERE TO GO?*

Everything you want to know about Parisian outings (theatre, cinema, restaurants, arts, music, visits and walks): www.premiere.fr

Pour connaître le programme des spectacles, adressez-vous à l' office du tourisme – qui vous réservera des places, si vous le leur demandez. Si vous êtes à Paris, achetez un journal spécialisé comme *Pariscope, l' Officiel des Spectacles* ou alors *Zurban*.

SORTIR LE SOIR *GOING OUT IN THE EVENING*

At the tourist office two tourists enquire about activities in the evening.

1 16.02 **Listen to the conversation and make a mental note of the activities that fit the tourists' taste.**

Touriste	Je passe quelques jours dans la région. Qu'est-ce qu'on peut faire ici le soir?
Hôtesse	Il y a beaucoup de choses à faire mais ça dépend, qu' est-ce que vous aimez? Le jazz? La danse?
Touriste	Oui, nous aimons danser mais surtout ... bien manger.
Hôtesse	Eh bien pourquoi n' allez-vous pas à un dîner-dansant ou dans un restaurant piano-bar?
Touriste	Un restaurant piano-bar, qu'est-ce que c'est?
Hôtesse	C' est un restaurant où il y a de la musique avec orchestre. En général, il y a une très bonne ambiance et ça reste ouvert toute la nuit. Mais ... si vous aimez danser, vous avez le restaurant 'Raspoutine' tout près d'ici qui organise des soirées dansantes avec repas et orchestre tzigane.
Touriste	C'est combien pour la soirée dansante?
Hôtesse	C'est 100 € par personne, tout compris, avec spectacle.
Touriste	Je peux acheter les billets ici?
Hôtesse	Non, il faut aller au restaurant qui se trouve au bout du boulevard Victor Hugo; mais ... attendez un instant, je vais vous chercher le programme des spectacles de la semaine avec la liste des restaurants et des bars.

In the first line of the dialogue the tourist says: '**Je passe quelques jours dans la région.**' The verb **passer** is very useful in statements and questions such as: **Je passe mes vacances..., Avez-vous passé de bonnes vacances? Comment avez-vous passé votre week-end?**

2 **Without looking back at the text say if the following statements are (V) vrai or (F) faux. Then correct the false answers:**
   a The tourist wants to know what's on in the daytime.
   b They like going to concerts.
   c A piano-bar is a place that is open only at lunchtime.
   d At 'Raspoutine' you can eat and dance.
   e The price for everything including the meal is 100€ per person.
   f The hostess gives the tourist the programme of the week.

3 **Here are the kinds of evening attractions described in a brochure that you can find at the tourist office. Read what is on at each nightspot and say who would enjoy which one most:**
   a A single lady who likes disco dancing – particularly older tunes – and would love to meet a male friend.
   b A couple who like playing bowls with their friends on Sundays.
   c A single person who likes betting and socializing on a regular basis.
   d A group of students who enjoy Latin music and dancing.
   e A man who enjoys tasting different types of beer, has a sweet tooth and likes music.

ACTIVITÉS NOCTURNES

1 Saxy Rock Café   Tél. 05 58 56 21 82
   Bar glacier
   5, avenue Milliès Lacroix
   Spécialités: bières du monde, glaces et pâtisseries,
   animations musicales.
   Ouvert tous les jours de 8h à 2h.

2 Havana Café
   Bar latino américain   Tél. 05 58 74 09 92
   19, rue Georges Chaulet
   Spécialités: cubaines. Ambiance salsa. Soirées concerts.
   Possibilité de location d' une salle pour soirée privée.
   Ouvert du mardi au dimanche à partir de 18h.

3 Casino de Dax   Tél. 05 58 56 86 86
   Avenue Milliès Lacroix
   Roulette, Black-jack, animations (spectacles, Calas),
   arts et culture, restaurant, bar.
   Ouvert tous les jours à partir de 15h.

4 César Palace
   Casino   Tél. 05 58 91 52 72
   Lac de Christus,
   40990 Saint-Paul-lès-Dax — 3 km Ouest
   **Boules le dimanche de 16h à 19h et tous les soirs
   de 22h à 4h. Machines à sous de 12h à 4h.**

5 Club rétro
   Le Richelieu — Club   Tél. 05 58 90 20 53
   Rue Sainte-Eutrope   ou 05 58 58 49 49
   Pour danser sur les souvenirs du temps passé.
   Entrée + consommation: 13€. Samedi: 15€
   (autres consommations: 10€).
   Ouvert du mercredi au dimanche à partir de 21h 30.
   Le mercredi entrée gratuite pour tous jusqu' à minuit.
   Le jeudi entrée gratuite pour les dames jusqu' à minuit.

4 16.03 **Listen to Michel booking a table by phone at the 'Burro Blanco' restaurant. Can you answer the following questions?**

> ### Espagnoles
>
> **BURRO BLANCO. 79, rue Cardinale Lemoine (5e)**
> **01 43 25 72 53.**
> Tlj jsq 5h du mat. F. Lun. À la Contrescarpe, véritable
> flamenco avec chanteurs, guitaristes et danseurs.
> Tapas. Menus 50€ à 60€. Carte.
>
> **GRENIER DE TRIANA, 7, rue Mouffetard (5e)**
> **01 43 57 97 33. Tls jsq 4h du mat.**
> La meilleure ambiance espagnole de Paris. Chants,
> guitare, paëlla, zarzuella. Menus 40€ à 70€ + Carte.
> Groupes.

a Which day is the restaurant shut?
b What special occasion is Michel celebrating?
c What does he ask for?
d What type of cooking is served?
e At what time does the show finish?
f What is included in the price?

5 **Using the Internet may be a useful way to find out what's on in the cinemas but abbreviated information can be a little confusing. How much can you decrypt in this example?**

> ## Cinéma Gaumont Opéra
> ## Impérial
>
> 29, bd des Italiens (2ème arr.)
>
> Métro/accès: Opéra
>
> Tél: 08.36.68.75.55
>
> Place 10€ 20
>
> Tarif réduit: 8€ 70 étud., CV, fam. nombr., mil., −18,
> du lun. au ven. 18h., sf. fêtes et veilles de fête
>
> Carte 5 places: 28€ 44

How well did you manage? Check your intuition by matching the abbreviations to their meaning.

a	bd	**1**	a discount card for senior citizens (**carte vermeil**)
b	arr.	**2**	large families (**familles nombreuses**)
c	étud.	**3**	underage minors
d	CV	**4**	except (**sauf**)
e	fam. nombr.	**5**	**boulevard**
f	mil.	**6**	municipal district (**arrondissement**)
g	-18	**7**	military personnel
h	sf	**8**	student

RÉSERVER UN COURT DE TENNIS *BOOKING A TENNIS COURT*

Une touriste veut jouer au tennis. Elle se renseigne à l'office du tourisme.

A tourist wants to play tennis. She enquires at the tourist office.

6 16.04 **Listen closely to the five questions she asks. Try to note at least three of them.**

Touriste	Où est-ce qu' on peut jouer au tennis?
Hôtesse	Vous avez à Anglet le Club de Chiberta avec 15 courts.
Touriste	Ah très bien, et où est-ce qu' on réserve les courts?
Hôtesse	Vous réservez les courts au club.
Touriste	C'est combien l'heure?
Hôtesse	Je ne sais pas. Il faut vous renseigner là-bas mais si vous jouez souvent, vous pouvez certainement prendre une carte d' abonnement.
Touriste	Je n'ai pas ma raquette de tennis avec moi. On peut louer une raquette au club?
Hôtesse	Je pense que oui.
Touriste	Vous pouvez me donner l' adresse du club, s' il vous plaît?
Hôtesse	Mais oui, la voilà.

7 How would you ask:

a Where can I play tennis? (use **on**)

b Where do I book the court? (use **on**)

c How much is it for one hour?

d Can one hire a racket? (use **on**)

e Can you give me the address of the club?

RÉSERVER UNE PLACE *BOOKING A TICKET*

8 16.05 **Listen to a student who is booking seats for a guitar recital. Why does she get a cheaper ticket?**

Jeune fille	Pardon Monsieur, je voudrais des places pour le récital de guitare, samedi prochain.
Employé	Je regrette, samedi c'est complet mais il reste encore des places pour jeudi et vendredi.
Jeune fille	Bon, eh bien je vais prendre deux places pour jeudi. Ça finit à quelle heure le concert?
Employé	Le concert commence à 19.45 donc je pense qu'il finira vers 22h.
Jeune fille	Bon, ça va, ce n'est pas trop tard. C'est combien la place, j'ai une carte étudiant?
Employé	Alors avec une carte étudiant, c'est tarif réduit à 20€60.
Jeune fille	Ma sœur a 15 ans. Elle doit payer?
Employé	C'est entrée libre jusqu'à 16 ans.

9 How do you say:

a I would like some seats for next Sunday.

b At what time does the concert finish?

c How much is it for a ticket?

d It is reduced rate.

e Does my sister have to pay?

10 You are working at the **office du tourisme** in Vittel. An English family comes in. They are all very eager to join in the various activities organized by the town (see the programme). Can you answer their questions?

● **ACTIVITÉS SPORTIVES ET DE LOISIRS avec JEAN-LOUIS et ANNE**

Jogging: dans le parc en petites foulées sur un rythme progressif.

Gymnastique: en salle, assouplissement et tonification musculaire.

Tir à l' arc: initiation et perfectionnement de la maîtrise du tir.

Promenades et randonnées (pédestre, vélo): parcourir la campagne et les bois environnants.

Self défense: initiation, découverte des gestes d'auto-défense.

Volley et sports collectifs. ✎

Gym, danse et stretching.

Promenade VTT: initiation. ✷ ✎

● **ACTIVITÉS TENNIS et GOLF avec BRUNO**

Usage des cours et du practice, du putting green. Initiation golf et tennis en groupe. ✎
Cours particuliers. ✷ ✎

● **L' OFFICE DU TOURISME EST À VOTRE DISPOSITION POUR** ses locations ou prêts de vélos, matériels de golf ✷, de tennis de table, jeux de société; son coin lecture (journaux, hebdomadaires).

> ✷ Activité avec participation financière.
> ✎ Activité avec inscription.

---

a The woman is very keen on playing tennis:
   1 Can she have private classes?
   2 Can she hire a tennis racket?

b The husband would like to go for a bicycle ride:
   1 Can he hire a bicycle?
   2 Does he need to enrol if he goes on an organized trip?

c Her youngest son would like to try out mountain biking
   (**VTT – vélo tous terrains**).
   1 Is it free?
   2 Does he need to enrol?

d Her daughter is very keen on doing archery. They have been told that the town runs archery classes:
   1 Is it true?
   2 Does she have to pay?

e If it rains, what can they do indoors?
   1 _____
   2 _____

Test yourself

1 **What questions would you ask to get these answers?**

   a On peut faire beaucoup de choses ici. Quels divertissements préférez-vous?

   _____

   b Non, il reste encore des places pour le concert de ce soir.

   _____

   c C'est 16€ de l'heure pour les courts de tennis, et 25€ pour deux heures.

   _____

   d Oui, on peut louer tout l'équipement de golf au club.

   _____

   e Alors, comme jeux de société il y a un Scrabble, un Monopoly et un Cranium.

2 **Can you complete the expressions with the words from the box.**

> abonnement   location   société   réduit
> à vélo   pédestre   particulier   dansante

   a une randonnée _____
   b une carte d' _____
   c une promenade _____
   d une soirée _____
   e un cours _____
   f un jeu de _____
   g un bureau de _____
   h tarif _____

SELF CHECK

I CAN. . .
. . . find out what's on at night.
. . . book tickets for a concert.
. . . ask where you can play tennis and other sports.

L'argent
Money

In this unit you will learn how to:
▶ *ask for change.*
▶ *recognize French coins and notes.*
▶ *learn to say that there is an error in a bill.*

Before you start, revise:
▶ *saying precisely what you want (Unit 7, Section 2).*
▶ *asking for help (Unit 9, Section 1).*
▶ *expressions of time, days of the week (Unit 5, Vocabulary builder).*
▶ *numbers (Units 2–6).*

La banque et l'euro

En **région parisienne** (*greater Paris area*), les banques sont principalement ouvertes du lundi au vendredi de 10 à 17h. En **province** (*the regions outside Paris*), elles ouvrent du mardi au samedi et ferment pendant une heure et demie entre 13 et 15h.

L'euro est **la devise nationale** (*national currency*) de la France et aujourd'hui de dix-sept autres pays membres de l'Union européenne. Il y a sept **billets** (*banknotes*) de couleurs et de tailles différentes: 5, 10, 20, 50, 100, 200 et 500€. Sur les billets on peut voir au recto des **fenêtres** (*windows*) et **portails** (*gates*), et au verso des **ponts** (*bridges*). Ces éléments illustrent différentes périodes de la culture européenne et forment des symboles d'ouverture et de coopération.

Where do banks close for lunchtime in France?
Which three motifs can be found on Euro banknotes?
What do they symbolize?

The Euro 'made in France'

Il y a huit **pièces** (*coins*): 1, 2, 5, 10, 20, 50 centimes, 1€, 2€. Dans un euro il y a 100 centimes. Chaque pièce a deux faces. La première est européenne. Commune avec les autres pays membres de l'Union, elle représente la valeur en euro et douze étoiles, symbole de l'Europe. La deuxième est nationale. Propre à chaque pays, elle représente les symboles caractéristiques de chaque pays. Sur la face française sont représentés trois symboles: la Marianne, symbole de la liberté et de la République, la Semeuse (*sower*), symbole de la fécondité, et l'Arbre, symbole de la vie.

1 **Answer these questions based on the passage.**

    a Are euro coins the same throughout the EU?

    b In what ways do they differ?

    c What is a fraction of a euro called?

2 **Look at these denominations of the euro. Some are real and some are fanciful. Can you identify the three that do not exist?**

    a une pièce de deux centimes

    b une pièce de soixante-quinze centimes

    c un billet de vingt euros

    d une pièce de cinq euros

    e un billet de mille euros

> **MIND THE DIFFERENCE!**
>
> The French use a comma to mark the decimal unit's position and the decimal point to separate sequences of three digits. However, English-speaking countries use the decimal point as the comma is already used to separate sequences of three digits, e.g.: £2,500.15; €3.000,45.

Vocabulary builder

3 17.01 **Listen and try to imitate the pronunciation of the speakers.**

L'ARGENT *MONEY*

une pièce	*coin*
un billet	*banknote*
un euro	*a euro*
la monnaie	*small change, currency*
la devise étrangère	*foreign currency*
la livre (sterling)	*pound (sterling)*
le dollar	*dollar*

POUR PARLER D'ARGENT *MONEY TALK*

le taux de change	*exchange rate*
la commission	*service charge*
un changeur de monnaie	*coin changing machine*
la carte bleue	*the French banker's card*
une carte bancaire	*banker's card*
la note	*hotel bill*
l'addition (f)	*bill (drinks, snacks)*
régler	*to settle (bill)*
une erreur	*a mistake*
le chiffre	*number*
un distributeur automatique	*a cashpoint*

POUR UTILISER L'ARGENT *USING MONEY*

Vous pouvez changer ... euros?	*Can you change ... euros?*
Vous avez de la monnaie, svp?	*Do you have any change please?*
Il me faut des pièces de 1€.	*I need 1€ coins.*
changer de l'argent	*change some money*
retirer de l'argent	*to withdraw money*
L'appareil ne rend pas la monnaie.	*This machine does not give change.*
La livre est à combien?	*What's the rate of exchange for the pound?*
Vous acceptez les cartes de crédit?	*Do you accept credit cards?*

How would you ask: *Can you change 10€, please?* And how would you say: *I need two 2€ coins?*

FAIRE DE LA MONNAIE *GETTING SMALL CHANGE*

4 17.02 **Listen to the conversation between a passer-by and a motorist, who needs some small change for the pay-and-display machine.**

Femme	Pardon, Madame, vous pouvez changer mon billet de 5€, s'il vous plaît?
Passante	Je ne sais pas, mais je vais regarder. Qu'est-ce qu'il vous faut?
Femme	C'est pour l'horodateur. Il me faut cinq pièces de 1€, ou alors une pièce de 1€ et deux pièces de 2€.
Passante	La machine ne rend pas la monnaie?
Femme	Non, et elle n'accepte que des pièces de 50 centimes, 1€ et 2€.
Passante	Et vous n'avez pas de carte bancaire?
Femme	Euh, non, je n'en ai pas.
Passante	Eh bien, vous avez de la chance! J'ai quatre pièces de 1€ et deux pièces de 50 centimes. Ça vous va?
Femme	Merci beaucoup, Madame.

ne … que	*only*
vous avez de la chance	*you're in luck*
ça vous va?	*is that OK (for you)?*

5 Find the French for the following phrases from the dialogues:

    a don't you have a bank card?
    b I need five coins of 1€
    c it only accepts …
    d can you change …?
    e I haven't got any (card)
    f I don't know
    g Is that OK?
    h you're lucky
    i I am going to see

6 **A businessman needs to take his young daughter to a pay toilet. He does not carry exact change and stops a woman on the street. Read the conversation, then answer the questions.**

Homme	Pardon madame, avez-vous de la monnaie pour les toilettes? Ma fille a un besoin urgent, et...
Passante	Qu'est-ce qu'il vous faut?
Homme	Vingt centimes, et je n'ai que cinq euros sur moi.
Passant	Je suis désolée mais j'ai seulement quelques pièces. Je n'ai pas la monnaie pour cinq euros. Tenez, voici vingt centimes.
Homme	C'est gentil de votre part, merci Madame.
Homme	Il n'y a pas de quoi. Vous savez, moi aussi j'ai des enfants alors je vous comprends.

a Can the woman change a 5€ note?

b What does she do to help the man?

c How does she justify her action?

> **C'est gentil de votre part.**
> *It's kind of you.*
> **Je n'ai que ... sur moi.**
> *I only have ... on me.*

CHANGER DE L'ARGENT *CHANGING MONEY*

7 Complete the text with the words from the box.

voyage	devises	change	bureaux	bancaire

On trouve de nombreux (**a**) _____ de change dans les grandes villes (gares, aéroports, grandes agences de banque, points de change). Les grandes postes changent aussi les (**b**) _____ étrangères et les chèques de (**c**) _____. Leurs taux de (**d**) _____ sont souvent meilleurs qu'ailleurs. Les distributeurs automatiques de billets (DAB) sont faciles d'accès partout en France. On y retire de l'argent avec une carte (**e**) _____, la carte Visa/Carte Bleue étant la plus acceptée en France suivie de MasterCard (Eurocard).

8 Follow the prompts and take part in this conversation in le bureau de change at the Gare du Nord in Paris.

You   *Say that you would like to change some dollars.*

Employé Des dollars américains, canadiens, australiens?

You   *Say American dollars.*

Employé D'accord. Vous voulez changer des billets ou des travellers?

You   *Say bank notes.*

Employé Combien voulez-vous changer?

You   *Say 200 dollars. Ask what the exchange rate is today.*

Employé Le dollar est à 0,82 aujourd'hui.

You   *Ask if there is a service charge.*

Employé Non, c'est inclus dans le taux de change. Voici votre argent, 164€.

17.03 **Now listen to the dialogue and check your answers.**

POUR RÉGLER LA NOTE *PAYING YOUR HOTEL BILL*

It's a good idea to ask for the bill in advance in order to check it.

You ask for **la note** to pay for your hotel bill and for **l'addition** to pay for food and drink.

Remember to check the price of hotel rooms which, by law, should be displayed at the reception and in each room.

Extras (telephone, mini-bar, etc.) should be charged separately.

TTC (toutes taxes comprises) means *inclusive of tax.*

TVA (taxe à la valeur ajoutée) means *VAT.*

9 17.04 **Here is some extra practice to help you cope with French prices. Listen to Michel and write down the prices you hear.**

a _____

b _____

c _____

d _____

e _____

f _____

g _____

h _____

i _____

j _____

UNE ERREUR DANS LA NOTE *AN ERROR IN THE BILL*

Un client s'apprête à quitter l'hôtel. Il trouve une erreur dans la note qu'il a demandée.

A guest is about to leave the hotel. Having asked for the bill, he spots a mistake.

10 17.05 **Listen to his conversation with the receptionist, then answer the questions.**

a What mistake was made on the bill?

Guest	Je voudrais régler ma note, s'il vous plaît.
Réceptionniste	Bien, vous partez aujourd'hui?
Guest	Oui, après le petit déjeuner.
Réceptionniste	Bon, c'est pour quelle chambre?
Guest	Chambre quatorze. Vous acceptez les cartes de crédit?
Réceptionniste	Oui, bien sûr. Alors un instant ... nous allons vérifier. Si vous voulez bien repasser après votre petit déjeuner votre note sera prête.
After breakfast...	
Guest	Pardon, Madame, il y a une erreur. Qu'est-ce que c'est 'mini-bar 10€'?
Réceptionniste	Ce sont les boissons du mini-bar que vous avez consommées dans votre chambre.
Guest	Mais je n'ai rien pris du mini-bar.
Réceptionniste	Vraiment? Bon, eh bien c'est sans doute une erreur de notre part...! Nous avons dû nous tromper de chambre. Je m'excuse Monsieur. Donc ça fait 94€ moins 10€ pour la boisson ... euh 84€.
Guest	C'est avec service et taxes?
Réceptionniste	Oui, taxes de séjour et service sont compris.

b When does the client intend to leave the hotel?

c What was the number of his room?

d What does the amount of 10€ correspond to?

e Is the bill inclusive of tax and service?

> **que vous avez consommées**
> *that you've drunk*
> **je n'ai rien pris**
> *I haven't taken anything*
> **nous avons dû nous tromper**
> *we must have made a mistake*

? Test yourself

1 **Match up the words in the left-hand column with the correct English translation in the right-hand column.**

a	la monnaie	**1**	banknote
b	un changeur de monnaie	**2**	banker's card
c	un distributeur automatique	**3**	bill (drinks, snacks)
d	une carte bancaire	**4**	exchange rate
e	la pièce	**5**	coin changing machine
f	un billet	**6**	a cashpoint machine
g	le taux de change	**7**	means of identification
h	l'addition	**8**	bill (hotel)
i	la note	**9**	coin
j	la pièce d'identité	**10**	small change

2 **Match the questions and the answers.**

a	Vous pouvez me faire de la monnaie sur 10€?	**1**	Aujourd'hui c'est 0,78 livre ou 1,23 dollars.
b	Est-ce qu'il faut payer une commission?	**2**	Désolé, mais je n'ai rien sur moi.
c	Avez-vous de la monnaie, s'il vous plaît?	**3**	Oui, deux billets de 5€, ça vous va?
d	Il y a une erreur dans ma note.	**4**	Oui, c'est 3,50€ par transaction.
e	L'euro est à combien?	**5**	Ah bon? Eh bien nous allons vérifier.

SELF CHECK

	I CAN...
●	. . . ask for change.
●	. . . recognize French coins and notes.
○	. . . say that there is an error in a bill.

18 Savoir faire face
Troubleshooting

In this unit you will learn how to:
▶ *ask for medicine at the chemist's.*
▶ *understand the French health system.*
▶ *make an appointment with the doctor/dentist.*
▶ *use key expressions to describe your problems.*

Before you start, revise:
▶ *saying precisely what you want (Unit 7, Section 2).*
▶ *how to describe things (Unit 7, Section 3).*
▶ *how to spell in French (Unit 12, Activity 8).*
▶ *how to say my, your, his, etc. (Unit 4, Section 7).*
▶ *expressions of time, days of the week (Unit 5, Vocabulary builder).*

La pharmacie en France

The French chemist's is easily recognizable, with its green neon cross sign outside. For minor ailments you'll find that the trained *pharmacist*, **pharmacien(-ne)** is usually happy to give you advice. Don't be afraid to ask the pharmacists for their advice. They will do it willingly as they see it as part of the services they offer their customers. You will not be able to buy medicines (even aspirin!) anywhere except at the **pharmacie**.

Pharmacie

Vocabulary builder

1 18.01 **Listen to the vocabulary and try to imitate the voice of the speakers.**

ASSISTANCE MÉDICALE *MEDICAL HELP*

la pharmacie	*chemist's*
le pharmacien, la pharmacienne	*chemist/pharmacist*
chez le médecin	*at the doctor's*
chez le dentiste	*at the dentist's*
le cabinet médical/dentaire	*doctor's/dentist's surgery*
prendre rendez-vous	*to make an appointment*
Je voudrais une consultation.	*I would like a doctor's appointment.*
passer voir	*come (go) and see*
une visite du docteur	*a home visit from the doctor*
souffrir	*to suffer, be in pain, feel ill*
depuis quand	*since when*
Je voudrais quelque chose pour...	*I would like something for...*
* les piqûres d'insectes	*insect bites*
le mal de gorge	*sore throat*
le mal de dents	*toothache*
le mal de tête	*headache*
J'ai mal à la gorge.	*I've got a sore throat.*
J'ai mal aux dents.	*I've got a toothache.*
J'ai mal à la tête.	*I've got a headache.*
J'ai mal au ventre.	*I've got stomach ache.*
Elle a la grippe.	*She's got flu.*
Il a de la fièvre.	*He's got a temperature.*

What French expression means *I've got an ache*?

ORDONNANCE *PRESCRIPTION*

je vous conseille	*I advise you, I recommend to you*
quelque chose contre le soleil	*something to prevent sunburn*
un médicament	*medicine*
une crème solaire	*sun cream*
une huile	*oil*
une crème anti-démangeaisons	*anti-itching cream*
une aspirine effervescente	*soluble aspirin*
en comprimés	*in tablet form*
des pastilles	*throat lozenges*
le dentifrice	*toothpaste*

À LA PHARMACIE *AT THE CHEMIST'S*

2 18.02 **Listen to the conversation between a chemist and a customer. Then answer the questions.**

a What's wrong with the customer's husband?

b Has he got a temperature?

c Name at least three items the customer buys.

Pharmacien	Bonjour, Madame. Vous désirez?
Cliente	Vous avez quelque chose pour le mal de gorge?
Pharmacien	C'est pour vous, Madame?
Cliente	Non, c'est pour mon mari.
Pharmacien	Il a de la fièvre?
Cliente	Non, mais il a aussi mal à la tête.
Pharmacien	Bon, pour le mal de gorge je vous donne des pastilles. Il en prend une quand il a mal. Pour le mal de tête, je vous donne de l'aspirine effervescente, deux comprimés toutes les quatre heures. Il n'est pas allergique à l'aspirine?
Cliente	Non, non ... merci. Je voudrais aussi du dentifrice et quelque chose contre le soleil.
Pharmacien	Vous préférez une crème ou une huile?
Cliente	Une crème.
Pharmacien	Alors voici du dentifrice et une crème pour le soleil; c'est tout?
Cliente	Oui, merci.
Pharmacien	Bon, eh bien ça fait 38€15.

3 Read the dialogue again and choose the right answers for the patient's medical record card below.

a	Patient complains of		b	Temperature
1	stomach-ache	☐		
2	headache	☐	Yes	☐
3	toothache	☐		
4	sore throat	☐	No	☐
c	**Treatment**		**d**	**To be taken**
1	antibiotics	☐		....
2	suppositories	☐		....
3	aspirin	☐		....
4	pastilles	☐		....

4 Now it's your turn to go to the chemist's to get some medicine for your daughter, who has a toothache. Follow the prompts.

Pharmacienne	Bonjour, Monsieur/Madame. Vous désirez?
You	*Say: my daughter has toothache.*
Pharmacienne	Elle a de la fièvre?
You	*Say: yes, a little.*
Pharmacienne	Depuis quand souffre-t-elle?
You	*Say: since yesterday.*
Pharmacienne	Bon, je vais vous donner de l'aspirine vitaminée et si ça continue dans un jour ou deux il faudra aller chez le dentiste.
You	*Thank her. Ask for something for insect bites.*
Pharmacienne	Pour les piqûres d'insectes? Certainement. Je vous conseille cette crème anti-démangeaisons ... elle est très efficace...
You	*Say: I'll take it and ask how much it is.*

 18.03 Now listen to the same conversation and check your answers.

LE SERVICE MÉDICAL *MEDICAL TREATMENT*

Before leaving for france

If you are a EU resident, remember to take your European Health Insurance Card (EHIC) with you. It can be obtained online (www.nhs.uk/nhsengland/Healthcareabroad). With the EHIC you can obtain a refund of generally 70 per cent on the cost of prescriptions and standard doctors' and dentists' fees.

Before making an appointment with a doctor or dentist, make sure that the practitioners are **conventionnés** (*charging the official social security rate*).

Show the doctor (general practitioners and specialists) your EHIC before paying him/her directly. He/She will fill out a **feuille de soins** (*treatment form*) and **une ordonnance** (*prescription*) if necessary.

You can buy your medication from any chemist's shop/pharmacy on presenting the **feuille de soins** and **ordonnance**. The chemist will give you a second **feuille de soins** displaying the price of the medicine and the **vignettes** (*stickers*) removed from the medicine packaging.

Once you have dated and signed the **feuilles de soins** and filled in your permanent address and bank details (name of bank, address, SWIFT code, account number and IBAN or BIC), you should send the forms to the nearest *Sickness Insurance Office* (**Caisse Primaire d'Assurance-Maladie** or **CPAM**) while you are still in France, together with the prescription and a copy of your European Health Insurance Card. The refund will be sent to your home address later. This refund process normally takes around two months.

Who issues the ordonnance, the doctor or the chemist? Which document gets sent to the Insurance Office for reimbursement?

CHEZ LE DOCTEUR *AT THE DOCTOR'S*

5 18.04 **Mrs Jones phones Dr Leroux's surgery to make an appointment. Listen to the conversation, then answer the questions.**

a Is Mrs Jones calling for herself or for someone else?

b What flu symptom does Mrs Jones describe?

c What's the difference between **une consultation** and **une visite**?

Réceptionniste	Allô, le cabinet du docteur Leroux, j'écoute.
Mrs Jones	Je voudrais prendre rendez-vous, s'il vous plaît.
Réceptionniste	Bon, c'est pour une consultation ou une visite?
Mrs Jones	Je ne comprends pas, vous pouvez expliquer?
Réceptionniste	Pour une consultation vous venez ici, pour une visite le médecin va chez vous. Vous êtes la patiente?
Mrs Jones	Non, c'est ma fille. Elle a beaucoup de fièvre...
Réceptionniste	Alors, vous voulez une visite ... Écoutez, le docteur est pris toute la journée mais il pourrait passer voir votre fille dans la soirée vers ... peut-être 19.30. Qu'est-ce qu'elle a, votre fille?
Mrs Jones	Je ne sais pas, peut-être la grippe. Elle a très mal à la tête.
Réceptionniste	Vous pouvez me donner votre nom et adresse?
Mrs Jones	Jones. J-O-N-E-S et j'habite appartement 2, 10 rue Legrand, à côté de la piscine.
Réceptionniste	Bon, et bien Mme Jones, le docteur Leroux passera voir votre fille vers 19.30.
Mrs Jones	Merci beaucoup. Au revoir, Madame.

> In this dialogue the **réceptionniste** uses the words **la journée, la soirée** and not **le jour, le soir**. The common rule is that **journée, soirée,** and **année** emphasize the notion of duration whereas **jour, soir,** and **an** merely describe moments in time.

 What do you think is the meaning of the expression le docteur est pris toute la journée?

6 Which of the following expressions can be used on the phone to signal to the other party that you haven't understood and would like him or her to repeat?

   a Vous pouvez m'aider?

   b Vous pouvez parler plus lentement?

   c Je ne comprends pas.

   d Vous pouvez m'appeler?

   e Vous pouvez répéter, s'il vous plaît?

   f Vous pouvez expliquer?

   g Je ne sais pas.

7 This conversation about making an emergency appointment at the dentist's is all jumbled up. Can you put it back in order, starting with 1.

_____	**a** Oui, bien sûr. C'est pour vous?
_____	**b** C'est une urgence. Alors ce matin, si possible, ou cet après-midi?
__1__	**c** Allô, Cabinet Dentaire Molaire, bonjour.
_____	**d** Douze ans.
_____	**e** Allô, bonjour madame. Je voudrais prendre rendez-vous.
_____	**f** Non, c'est pour mon fils. Il a mal aux dents depuis jeudi.
_____	**g** Cet après-midi à 15.45. Ça vous va?
__5__	**h** Et il a quel âge votre fils?
_____	**i** C'est très bien, merci Madame. Et à cet après-midi.
_____	**j** Oui, je vois. Et quand peut-il venir?

18.05 **Did you manage to reconstruct the dialogue? Listen to check your answers.**

AU COMMISSARIAT DE POLICE *AT THE POLICE STATION*

Pour tout papier d'identité perdu ou volé, vous devez faire une déclaration (*statement*) au commissariat de police (*police station*) le plus proche. Vous pouvez aussi informer votre consulat. Pour un objet personnel perdu à Paris, présentez-vous en personne au 36, rue des Morillons, 15ème. Pour une carte de crédit, faites une déclaration au commissariat de police après avoir téléphoné au service d'urgence de votre carte.

PERTES ET VOLS *LOSSES AND THEFT*

J'ai perdu (il a perdu)...	*I've lost (he's lost)*
la perte	*loss*
J'ai laissé (il a laissé)...	*I've left (he's left)...*
...est cassé(e)	*...is broken*
...sont cassés(ées)	*...are broken*
On a volé...	*...was stolen*
le vol	*theft*
le sac à main	*handbag*
le portefeuille	*wallet*
le porte-monnaie	*purse*
les lunettes	*glasses*
remplir un formulaire/imprimé	*fill in a form*
faire une déclaration par écrit	*to make a statement in writing*

8 18.06 **Listen to Michel's various mishaps and fill in the blanks using the correct items from the box.**

identité	faire	voiture	cartes	telephone
portefeuille	lunettes	clés	stylo	

a Hier matin, j'ai perdu mes _____ d'appartement dans le métro.

b Après ça, j'ai laissé mon _____ en or et mes _____ à la banque.

c Juste avant midi, on m'a volé au restaurant mon _____ avec tout mon argent et mes _____ de crédit.

d Hier soir, j'ai oublié au commissariat de police ma carte d'_____ et mon parapluie tout neuf.

e Ce matin, j'ai téléphoné au commissariat, mais personne ne m'a répondu. Je crois que mon _____ est cassé.

f Alors j'ai pris ma _____, mais je ne comprends pas, elle ne démarre plus. Mais qu'est-ce que je vais _____?

9 18.07 **A man is at the police station reporting the theft of his car. Can you give the make, colour and number plate of his car?**

Agent	Monsieur?
Homme	Je suis anglais, en vacances avec ma famille ... On m'a volé ma voiture.
Agent	Quand ça?
Homme	La nuit dernière.
Agent	Où était votre véhicule?
Homme	Ma voiture? Dans la rue Gambetta devant l'hôtel du Lion d'Or.
Agent	C'est quoi votre voiture?
Homme	C'est une Volvo S70 rouge.
Agent	Quel est le numéro d'immatriculation?
Homme	Euh ... AB08 PLM.
Agent	Bon, nous allons essayer de la retrouver. En attendant, il faut faire une déclaration par écrit. Vous pouvez remplir cet imprimé?
Homme	Euh ... maintenant?
Agent	Oui, tout de suite car vous en avez besoin pour vos assurances en Angleterre; mais c'est facile ... c'est traduit en anglais.

10 Read the dialogue again and try to spot the French version of the following phrases:
  a my car was stolen
  b what make of car is it?
  c what's the registration number?
  d write a statement
  e fill in this printed form
  f you need it for your insurance

était	*was*
en attendant	*in the meantime*

?? Test yourself

1 Match the two parts of the sentences.

a J'ai mal à...   1 ventre.
b Tu n'as pas...   2 aux dents.
c J'ai mal au...   3 de fièvre.
d Elle a mal...   4 pastilles pour la gorge.
e Nous prenons des...   5 la tête.

2 You have caught a stomach bug whilst on holiday abroad. You need to see a doctor and ring a medical practice to make arrangements.

a Say that you want an appointment with the doctor.

_____

b Explain that your belly hurts.

_____

c Say that you have been suffering for three days.

_____

d Say that you cannot eat.

_____

e Tell the receptionist that you can come tomorrow morning at ten o'clock.

_____

3 Choose the correct verb and/or verb form to complete the sentences.

a Hier matin, j'ai perdu/volé mes lunettes dans le bus.
b Elle a pris/laissé son parapluie à la maison.
c On m'ai volé/a volé ma voiture!
d Mes lunettes est cassée/sont cassées.
e Tu as oublié/oubliez ton passeport dans l'avion.

SELF CHECK

I CAN...

⚫	... ask for medicine at the chemist's.
⚫	... understand the French health system.
⚫	... make an appointment with the doctor/dentist.
⚪	... use key expressions to describe my problems.

Answer key

UNIT 1

Vous parlez français?

b répondez

Vocabulary builder

Greetings: good night, goodbye
New expressions: yes…, thank you.., please, what about you?

Conversation

1 a They say bonsoir, so it's the evening. **b** Messieurs-dames, **c** Comment vas-tu? **d** Comment allez-vous?
When things get difficult: 3 in a café **4** 3**a** 2**b** 4**c** 1**d** **5** parlez, regrette, bien, moi, qu'est-ce que
When to use tu/vous: a tu, **b** vous, **c** tu, **d** vous, **e** vous

Practice

1 c **2 a** Bonjour, Madame/Mademoiselle **b** Bonjour, Monsieur **c** Bonsoir, Madame/Mademoiselle **d** Bonjour, Messieurs-dames **e** Bonne nuit, Monsieur **f** Bonne nuit, Messieurs-dames **3** Bonsoir, Monsieur **4** Bonne nuit **5** Comment ça va? Très bien, merci. **6 a** s'il vous plaît **b** ça va **c** au revoir **d** madame **e** bonsoir **f** non merci **7 a** 3, **b** 2, **c** 3, **d** 3, **e** 2

Test yourself

1 a nuit, **b** bien, **c** allez, **d** beaucoup **2 a** je vais bien, et toi? **b** qu'est-ce que vous désirez? **c** comment allez-vous, Monsieur?

UNIT 2

French café bars

le/l' for *the*, **des/de** for *some*

Vocabulary builder

Au café du coin: one coffee, one tea, (still) water, (some) lemonade, (some) sandwiches, (the) postcard, (the) toilets
Numbers 1–10: the **p** is not pronounced.

Conversation

1 a some beer and wine, two bottles of mineral water **b** No, there isn't any beer. **2 a** deux bouteilles d'eau, **b** C'est tout?, **c** C'est combien?

Language discovery

the

Practice

1 a un café **b** une bière **c** un journal **d** des bouteilles **e** un euro **f** un timbre **2** les toilettes, un café, l'addition **3 a** Je voudrais quatre cartes postales, s'il vous plaît **b** Vous_avez quatre timbres...? **c** Et de l'aspirine, s'il vous plaît. **d** C'est combien? **4 a** c'est combien la bouteille d'eau? **b** je voudrais une limonade. **c** avez-vous des sandwiches? **d** c'est un euro trente.

Listen and understand

1 a Messieurs-dames **b** café **c** bière **d** voudrais **e** addition **2 a** cinq **b** neuf **c** dix **d** neuf **e** deux **f** quatre **g** neuf **h** huit

Test yourself

1 a 2, **b** 4, **c** 1, **d** 3 **2** trois

UNIT 3

Family ties

I am a girl, I have a daughter

Vocabulary builder

La famille: brother, father, grandparents, grandmother, a girlfriend

Conversation

1 a Yes, they both have a job. **b** Jane is English and Irish. **c** She has three: a girl and two boys. **d** No, she's not married. **e** She's a dentist. **2 a** T **b** F **c** F **d** T

Language discovery

je travaille, tu travailles, il travaille, nous travaillons, vous travaillez, elles travaillent

4 the number 19. **Dix** is followed by the consonant **n**, but it is still sounded as **z**.

Practice

1 a 13 **b** 18 **c** 4 **d** 12 **e** 7 **f** 19 **g** 5 **h** 15 **i** 11 **j** 9 **2 a** treize **b** vingt **c** dix-neuf **d** onze **e** six **f** douze **3 a** n'est pas marié **b** n'est pas secrétaire **c** n'ont pas d'enfants **d** n'est pas dans le nord de l'Angleterre **e** ne parle pas français **f** n'a pas 18 ans

Reading

1 a est **b** ont **c** Elles **d** enfants, un **e** n'a pas **f** n'est pas **g** frère **h** est **2 a** He's an accountant. **b** She works in advertising. **c** Anne is a part-time secretary.

Test yourself

1 a Vous travaillez? **b** Vous_ êtes marié? **c** Vous_avez des_enfants? **d** Ils_ont quel âge? **2 a** 4 **b** 3 **c** 2 **d** 1 **3 a** Elle est américaine **b** Tu n'as pas une amie anglaise **c** Elle est mariée **d** Elles travaillent dans une agence de voyages.

REVIEW 1 (UNITS 1–3)

1 a 5, **b** 3, **c** 4, **d** 2, **e** 1 **2 a** douze **b** neuf **c** treize **d** dix-huit **e** quatorze **3 a** Et vous, vous travaillez dans une banque? **b** Vous_avez des_enfants? **c** Vous_êtes mariée? **d** Vous parlez français et anglais, non? **e** Répètez, s'il vous plaît. **4 a** suis **b** est **c** sont **d** ai **e** sont **f** a **g** ont **h** avons **i** sommes **j** ai **5 a** Je ne comprends pas. **b** Elle n'a pas de bière. **c** Vous n'habitez pas Londres. **d** Ils n'ont pas trois enfants. **e** Elle n'est pas professeure.

6 a Comment_allez-vous? **b** Ils_habitent Paris? **c** Comment vous_appelez-vous? **d** Vous_êtes français? **e** Vous parlez_anglais? **f** Vous_avez des_enfants? **g** Vous travaillez? **h** Elle est mariée avec Martin? **i** C'est combien, la baguette? **j** Quel âge as-tu?

UNIT 4

Suburban life

hommes, femmes; Do you live in Paris or in the suburbs?

Vocabulary builder

a loin / près , **b** grande / petite, **c** cher / bon marché, **d** ouvert / fermé

Conversation

a Yes, in Chatou, 45 minutes away, **b** three, two girls and a boy, **c** she's a teacher, **d** no, Jane is in France on holiday.

Language discovery

Il y a une pharmacie à Chatou?, C'est loin le cinéma?

Practice

1 a 5 **b** 2 **c** 1 **d** 4 **e** 3 **2** (Note that there are alternative ways of asking these questions) **a** Il y a un restaurant dans l'hôtel? **b** Il y a une pharmacie près d'ici? **c** Il y a des magasins près d'ici? **d** La banque est ouverte? **e** Il y a un train direct pour Paris? **f** C'est loin la gare? **3 a** Il y a une pharmacie mais_il n'y a pas d'aspirine **b** Il y a une pâtisserie mais_il n'y a pas de croissants **c** Il y a une gare mais_il n'y a pas de trains **d** Il y a un arrêt d'autobus mais_il n'y a pas de bus **e** Il y a un bar mais_il n'y a pas de bière **f** Il y a une cabine téléphonique mais_il n'y a pas de téléphone **4 a** Vous_êtes en vacances? **b** Vous_êtes mariée? **c** Vous_avez des enfants? **d** Vous_habitez Londres? **e** Vous travaillez? **5 a** combien **b** où **c** quand **d** où **e** quoi **6 a** 49€50 **b** 3€75 **c** 8€60 **d** 56€15 **e** 68€ **8 a** sa, **b** leurs, **c** votre, **d** ton, **e** ma, **f** nos **9** 5, 1, 4, 3, 2 **10 a** son travail, **b** ses amies, **c** ses vacances, **d** sa banlieue, **e** son parc, **f** sa voiture, **11 a** grande, **b** cher, **c** fermés, **d** loin

Listening and speaking

1 missing words: français, petit, d'ici, lentement, à pied, **a** the French lady speaks too fast, **b** a chemist's, **c** it's nearby, only 10 minutes away. **2** Vous_êtes_en vacances?, Oui, mais_elle est fermée, Oui. C'est loin, mais l'arrêt d'autobus est au bout de la rue, C'est le bus (numéro) 27.

Test yourself

(Note that there are alternative ways of asking these questions)

1 a Vous vous_appelez comment? **b** Vous_habitez où? **c** Vous_avez des_ enfants? **d** Il y a une banque près d'ici? **e** C'est où, l'arrêt d'autobus? **2 a** Je n'ai pas d'enfants. **b** J'habite dans la banlieue de Paris. **c** Il y a beaucoup de magasins près d'ici. **d** La gare est à cinq minutes (d'ici). **e** Mes enfants travaillent à Paris. **3 a** neuf, vingt_et un, vingt-sept **b** huit, soixante-quatre **c** dix, quarante, soixante

UNIT 5

French attitude to time

Yes, **à huit heures et demie** is a precise time, **vers huit heures** is approximate.

Vocabulary builder

L'avion part quand? Le bus arrive quand? On rentre quand? On peut prendre le petit déjeuner quand? Il y a un métro quand? Le concert finit quand?

Conversation

a She has lunch at the school's cafeteria, **b** Tuesdays and Thursdays, **c** from Saturday noon to Monday morning

Les mois de l'année: March, April, May, September, October, November **Numbers 70-90:** soixante-dix, soixante-dix-huit, quatre-vingt-six, quatre-vingt-sept – The word **vingt** takes an **s** in 80 because it is not followed by another number.

Practice

1 a prends **b** commencent **c** arrive **d** apprend **e** déjeune **f** prenez **g** fais **h** est **i** finit **j** faites **k** attendons **l** comprennent **2 a** 3, **b** 7, **c** 5, **d** 1, **e** 2, **f** 4, **g** 6 **3** 3a, 8b, 4c, 6d, 2e, 1f, 5g, 7h **4 a** le 1er mai, **b** le 3 février, **c** le 21 mars, **d** le 15 juillet, **e** le 10 juin, **f** le 13 octobre, **g** le 30 septembre, **h** le 6 août **5 a** prends **b** prennent **c** commence **d** travaille **e** déjeune **f** finit **g** fait **h** regardent **6 a** mercredi **b** vendredi **c** dimanche **d** jeudi **7** Je prends le train à sept heures vingt; Je commence à neuf heures du matin; Je prends un café; Non, j'écoute un podcast. **8 a** il est neuf heures dix (du matin) **b** midi moins vingt **c** une heure et demie (de l'après-midi) **d** six heures vingt-cinq (du soir) **e** minuit moins dix

Test yourself

1 a lundi, mardi, mercredi, jeudi, vendredi, **b** janvier, février, mars, **c** le 1er janvier **2 a** comprenons, **b** finit, **c** regardez, **d** faites **3** a and b

UNIT 6

Asking your way

grand – **magasin** is a store, **grand magasin** is a department store, encore une fois?

Vocabulary builder

gauche, droite; **a** 3, **b** 1, **c** 4, **d** 2

Conversation

As you leave the house turn left, go to the end of rue Vaugirard, turn right into rue Vincennes and the park is 200 metres on your left. It takes approximately 25 minutes.

Language discovery

5 à + le, la, l', les: Je voudrais aller au cinéma. Vous allez au parc? Elles vont à la piscine le jeudi. Ma grand-mère va à l'hôpital. **6 Locating the exact spot:** C'est en face des grands magasins. Je suis au coin de la rue **Numbers over 90:** cent-quarante-neuf, trois mille **8 Premier, deuxième...:** le cinquième (étage), s'il vous plaît.

Practice

1 a Pour aller à la piscine? **b** Pour aller à la gare? **c** Pour aller à l'église St. Paul? **d** Pour aller au musée? **e** Pour aller à l'office du tourisme? **2 a** C **b** E **c** A **d** D **e** B **4 a** à Brighton, **b** en France, **c** l'Allemagne, **d** au Danemark, **e** aux_États-Unis / au Japon, **f** à Londres **5 a** en face du **b** à côté de la **c** au coin de **d** entre **e** au bout de **f** grands magasins **g** bar **h** pâtisserie **i** dans la rue **j** sur la place **7** La banque est à côté de la pharmacie. Ils sont_en face du supermarché. Il faut environ 15 minutes à pied. Elle est_en face du café. Non, elle est fermée, mais elle ouvre à 2 heures.

Test yourself

1 a 2, **b** 4, **c** 5, **d** 1, **e** 3 **2 a** quatre-vingt-treize, quatre-vingt-dix-neuf **b** cent vingt, cent cinq **c** soixante-dix, cent dix, **d** mille cent cinquante, mille quatre cent cinquante **3 a** 3, **b** 1, **c** 4, **d** 2, **e** 5

UNIT 7

The meaning of colours

a 5, **b** 4, **c** 3, **d** 6, **e** 1, **f** 7, **g** 8, **h** 2

Vocabulary builder

un peu

Conversation

a souvenir for her mum, **b** it's not as expensive, **c** a blue and red one

Language discovery

ces magasins, ces choses / J'ai beaucoup d'amis

Practice

1 cet, ces, ce, ces, ce, cet, cette, cette **2** Mme Durand a 35 ans. Elle a les cheveux blonds et longs. Elle a les_yeux verts. Elle fait 1,70 mètre et pèse 65 kg. Elle porte des lunettes rondes. Elle porte un ensemble vert uni, des chaussures légères et une chemise blanche. Jane a 23 ans. Elle a les cheveux bruns et courts. Ses_yeux sont bleus (Elle a les_yeux bleus). Elle fait 1,62 mètre et pèse 55 kg. Elle porte un jean bleu pâle et un pull-over blanc. Elle a (porte) des bottes noires. **3 a** Chère **b** famille **c** tout **d** sympathique **e** bonnes **f** grande/confortable **g** grande/confortable **h** longues **i** jours **j** meilleure **k** anglaise **l** mieux **m** prochaine **4 a** un grand café noir / deux pressions / et un petit crème / non, deux pressions, un petit crème et un grand café noir / Vous_avez des croissants? / J'en voudrais quatre **5 a** une boîte de petits pois français **b** une tarte aux pommes **c** un baba au rhum **d** une glace à la vanille **e** un sorbet au citron **f** un café au lait sans sucre **g** un poulet à 6€80 **h** un sandwich au fromage

Test yourself

1 bleu, noir, vert, blanc, marron, jaune, rouge **2 a** c'est un jeune homme sympathique. **b** elles ont les cheveux longs et blonds **c** ces lunettes noires sont trop chères, **d** mon vieil ami habite dans une grande ville **3 a** Je voudrais une boîte de haricots verts. **b** Un sandwich au fromage, s'il vous plaît. **c** Elle dépense plus que moi. **d** Le livre est meilleur que le film.

REVIEW 2 (UNITS 4–7)

1 a 5 **b** 4 **c** 1 **d** 3 **e** 2 **2 a** ouvert **b** midi **c** derrière **d** monter la rue **e** à droite **f** jamais **g** grand **h** homme **i** cheveux longs **j** vieilles **3 a** soixante et un **b** quarante-trois **c** quatre-vingts **d** quatre-vingt-quatorze **e** cent six **f** quatre mille **4 a** Il est neuf heures quarante-cinq. b Il est vingt-deux heures trente. c Il est treize heures vingt. d Il est six heures. **5 a** le dimanche trente et un mars **b** le mercredi deux juin **c** le vendredi dix-huit janvier, **d** le samedi onze mai **e** le jeudi dix-neuf septembre **6** Non, c'est la première fois/que je vais_à Paris. / Une semaine. / Non, j'ai des_amis américains/qui habitent Paris. / Il est journaliste/et elle ne travaille pas. / Ils_habitent dans le seizième arrondissement / près du Bois de Boulogne. / Non, les taxis sont trop chers.

UNIT 8

The most popular sports in France

football, tennis, horse riding, judo, and gymnastics; la pétanque; faire and jouer

Vocabulary builder

jouer au for sports and **jouer du** for instruments

Conversation

a cooking, **b** squash, swimming, windsurfing, **c** Mr Durand: he takes the children to the pool, **d** Yes, because she says she does most sports.

Language discovery

je joue de la flûte, je joue au golf, je joue au badminton, je fais de l'équitation / j'aime jouer du piano, j'adore jouer au golf, je n'aime pas regarder la télé, je déteste faire des courses **Pratiquez!**: je préfère la cuisine italienne nous n'aimons pas les films américains, ils adorent la musique reggae

Practice

1 a Comment vous_appelez-vous? Je m'appelle Roger Burru **b** Quel âge avez-vous? J'ai 35 ans **c** Vous_avez des_enfants? Non, je n'ai pas d'enfants **d** Qu'est-ce que vous faites dans la vie? Je suis professeur **e** Où habitez-vous? J'habite Lille **f** Qu'est-ce que vous faites comme sport? Je fais de la natation **g** Vous faites quoi pendant vos loisirs? J'aime beaucoup faire la cuisine **2** e, c, a adore, d, g aime beaucoup, f, h n'aime pas, b déteste **3 a** 6, **b** 4, **c** 3, **d** 2, **e** 7, **f** 8, **g** 1, **h** 5, **4 a** F **b** F **c** V **d** V **e** V **f** F **g** V **h** V **i** F **j** F **k** V **l** F

Go further

1 a 5 **b** 3 **c** 6 **d** 7 **e** 1 **f** 4 **g** 2 **2** Marlène fait de la danse et du théâtre, Ludovic fait du sport, de la peinture et de la photo, Séverine fait du bénévolat.

Test yourself

1 a j'adore jouer au tennis, **b** Vous aimez faire la cuisine? **c** Je n'écoute plus de la musique pop, **d** Je ne connais pas bien Paris, **e** Elle sait faire du ski.
2 a joue au, **b** fais de, **c** jouent à la **d** fais du **3 a** 3, **b** 4, **c** 2, **d** 1

UNIT 9

Dealing with problems

Le distributeur de billets est en panne. Mon portable ne marche pas.

Vocabulary builder

Ma ligne (de téléphone) est en dérangement/ne marche pas.

Conversation

a She doesn't know how to use the date-stamping machine **b** She suggests turning the ticket the right way round.

Language discovery

Vous pouvez me donner l'heure, s'il vous plaît? Vous pouvez parler plus lentement? / Qu'est-ce qu'il faut faire pour téléphoner en Grande-Bretagne? Il faut attendre le prochain train.

Practice

1 a 5, **b** 7, **c** 4, **d** 2, **e** 6, **f** 1, **g** 3 **2 a** 4, **b** 5, **c** 1, **d** 6, **e** 2, **f** 3 **3 a** 4 **b** 3 **c** 1 **d** 2
4 a 3 **b** 6 **c** 2 **d** 4 **e** 2 **f** 5 **5 a** 7 **b** add pepper and salt **c** 30 g of butter **d** when the butter is hot **e** a fork **6** 2-**a** 4-**b** 1-**c** 6-**d** 5-**e** 3-**f** 7 **7** Mon portable ne marche pas. Vous pouvez m'aider? / Je ne comprends pas. Vous pouvez parler plus lentement? / Non, vous pouvez me montrer comment faire, s'il vous plaît? / Merci de votre aide.

Go further

a il ne faut pas parler pendant le film **b** il est interdit/il est défendu de prendre des photos au flash dans le musée **c** il est interdit/il est défendu d'utiliser son téléphone dans l'avion **d** il est interdit/il est défendu de filmer le concert de rock en vidéo **e** il ne faut pas aller dans l'eau après manger **f** il est interdit/il est défendu de nourrir les animaux du zoo

Test yourself

1 a Je ne sais pas **b** Je ne comprends pas **c** Vous pouvez m'aider, s'il vous plaît? **d** La machine ne marche pas **e** Qu'est-ce qu'il faut faire? **f** Il me faut un passeport pour aller en France **g** Il faut boire beaucoup
2 a L'autobus est en panne, il faut prendre un taxi. The bus is broken down. We'll have to take a taxi. **b** D'abord tu fais fondre le beurre, et ensuite tu verses les oeufs. **c** Merci de votre aide. Il n'y a pas de quoi.

UNIT 10

Planning the holidays

prendre des vacances, **passer les** vacances; **rendre visite à** with people, **visiter** with places and attractions

Vocabulary builder

je vais (*I'm going*) and **je vais aller** (*I'm going to go*)

Conversation

a 4 weeks, **b** to the seaside and to the mountains, **c** Mrs Durand: swimming, play tennis, go for long walks and see regional historic monuments; Mr Durand: have a rest, read, do some sport (e.g. tennis), play pétanque, go to the cinema or restaurant. **d** No, she prefers to stay at home or go out to a nightclub with friends.

Language discovery

Pratiquez! je m'habille, tu t'habilles, il/elle/on s'habille, nous nous_ habillons, vous vous_habillez, ils s'habillent **2 Saying what you need…:** Nous avons soif, Avez-vous froid? Elle a toujours faim.

Practice

1 a 2, **b** 4, **c** 5, **d** 1, **e** 6, **f** 3 **2 a** je me lève à huit heures, **b** nous allons nous baigner cet après-midi, **c** ils prennent le petit déjeuner à l'hôtel, **d** en juillet elle passe trois semaines au bord de la mer, **e** vous allez louer une maison? **3 a** D'abord je me lève à 7 heures **b** puis je me lave **c** ensuite je prends le petit déjeuner avec les_enfants **d** À 8h30, j'emmène les_enfants à l'école **e** ensuite je fais des courses **f** À midi, je prépare le déjeuner **g** L'après-midi, je joue au tennis **h** ou je vais chez mes_amis **i** ou je vais au cinéma **j** Le soir, je regarde la télévision **k** ou j'écoute la radio **l** enfin je me couche à 23 heures. **4** Vous allez partir quand en vacances? Où allez-vous aller? Comment allez-vous passer vos vacances? **Robert:** en août / 3 semaines / visiter des monuments historiques / voir des_amis / sortir le soir / jouer au tennis. **Jeanine:** le 21 juin / 10 jours / lire beaucoup, regarder un peu la télévision / faire de longues promenades / me coucher tôt **5 a** fils **b** Grande-Bretagne **c** finit **d** samedi **e** rester **f** jours **g** visiter **h** besoin **i** prendre **6 a** j'y travaille **b** ils n'y vont jamais **c** vous y allez en hiver? **d** nous y allons souvent

Listening and speaking

1 a téléphoner à Marc **b** aller chez le dentiste **c** aller à la banque **d** faire des courses et acheter 2 steaks, une bouteille de vin et une glace à la fraise **e** jouer au tennis **f** faire la cuisine **g** inviter Anne à dîner **2** Je vais aller au Portugal, avec ma femme et mes deux enfants, nous_y allons pendant le mois d'août, nous_allons passer deux semaines au bord de la mer, les enfants vont jouer au tennis le matin et se baigner l'après-midi, nous_allons nous reposer et nous promener, nous_allons lire et parler avec nos amis, Oui, ils peuvent sortir en boîte avec leurs_amis.

Go further

1 a sortons, **b** viens, **c** sortent, **d** venons, **e** vient, **f** sort, **g** venez, **h** sortir

Test yourself

a nous nous levons à sept heures du matin, **b** Elle va visiter les monuments de Londres, **c** je dois acheter le journal **d** comment vas-tu passer tes vacances? **e** En été / L'été nous rendons visite à nos grands-parents, **f** je sors avec mes amis

REVIEW 3 (UNITS 8–10)

1 a Sophie déteste, Mohamed aime beaucoup jouer au football **b** Sophie aime beaucoup, Mohamed déteste faire la cuisine **c** Sophie aime beaucoup, Mohamed n'aime pas regarder la télévision **d** Sophie adore, Mohamed aime beaucoup écouter de la musique **e** Sophie n'aime pas, Mohamed adore faire de la natation **f** Sophie adore, Mohamed déteste faire du ski **g** Sophie n'aime pas, Mohamed aime beaucoup aller au restaurant **h** Sophie déteste, Mohamed adore jouer au tennis **2 a** me **b** t' **c** se **d** nous **e** vous **f** se **3 a** écoute **b** manges **c** travaillons **d** jouez **e** fait/pratique **4 a** il fait mauvais **b** il fait beau **c** le soleil brille **d** il fait chaud **e** il neige **f** il fait froid **g** il pleut **5 a** allez **b** allons **c** va **d** vas **e** vais **f** vont **6 a** passe **b** me promène **c** me baigne **d** sors **e** rendre **f** faire **7 a** 3, **b** 4, **c** 5, **d** 1, **e** 2, **8 a** D'abord il faut sélectionner un film. **b** Après ça il faut choisir l'heure du film. **c** Troisièmement on doit indiquer le nombre de personnes. **d** Ensuite il faut cliquer sur 'acheter'. **e** Puis on doit insérer son numéro de carte bancaire. **f** Et finalement, il faut noter le numéro de confirmation. **9 a** J'ai besoin de boire de l'eau. **b** J'ai besoin de demander l'addition. **c** J'ai besoin d'aller à la banque. **d** J'ai besoin de mettre un vêtement chaud. **e** J'ai besoin de porter mes lunettes de soleil. **f** J'ai besoin de manger un snack. **10** Je ne parle pas très bien français. / Vous pouvez parler plus lentement, s'il vous plaît? / Vous voulez venir quand au mois d'août? / Je suis vraiment désolée / mais je ne peux pas en août. / Je suis_au Canada du 20 juillet au 20 août. / Je voudrais beaucoup vous voir. / Vous pouvez changer les dates de vos vacances? Ces dates sont plus pratiques pour moi. / Oui. Vous pouvez acheter le billet. **11 a** J'ai perdu mon stylo en or au bureau. **b** Mon frère a perdu sa valise marron à l'aéroport. **c** Ma sœur a perdu son porte-monnaie en cuir blanc au parc. **d** Son père a perdu son passeport britannique dans la rue. **e** Mon amie a perdu son foulard en soie dans l'autobus.

UNIT 11

Les magasins en France

1 a 7/8 p.m. **b** shut **c** Monday **d** pâtisseries, charcuteries **2 a, c** boucherie, **d, e, g** épicerie, **b** boulangerie, **f** charcuterie **3** c, f, h, a, e, d, g, i, b

New expressions

Où est l'épicerie la plus proche? / Je cherche quelque chose de plus petit.

Conversation

4 a des fruits/fraises **b** de l'eau minérale **c** c'est un peu trop gros/c'est assez **5** b, d, g, l **6 a** je voudrais trois cents grammes de fromage, (s'il vous plaît). **b** Je vais prendre une demi-livre de fraises. **c** Pouvez-vous me donner un paquet de jambon? **d** C'est tout. C'est combien? **7 a** Pressing **b** Librairie **c** Informatique **d** Bijouterie **e** Chaussures **f** Lingerie – Vêtements **g** Traiteur/ Charcuterie **h** Cave – Marchand de Vin **8 a** un tire-bouchon **b** un maillot de bain **c** l'huile pour bronzer **d** les journaux **e** brosse à dent **9 a** 5, **b** 4, **c** 1, **d** 2, **e** 3, **10 a** Je cherche une jupe noire. **b** Elles font combien ces jupes? **c** quelque chose de moins cher **d** Vous acceptez les cartes de crédit? **11** Je voudrais un journal. Qu'est-ce que vous avez comme journaux anglais? / Je vais prendre *The Times* et ces trois cartes postales. C'est combien les timbres pour l'Angleterre?/ Bon, je vais prendre huit timbres. / Ah, et je vais aussi acheter le magazine *Elle* pour ma femme. **12 a** a jumper **b** white or pale yellow **c** it's too big **d** he doesn't like the colour **e** 68€50

Test yourself

1 a 4 What size are you? **b** 5 Don't you have something different? **c** 2 Where are the fitting rooms? **d** 1 I'll have 10 slices of ham. **e** 3 Are you being served? **2 a** trouver, **b** proche, **c** quelque **d** d'œufs **e** beurre **3 a** lait **b** pomme de terre **c** pain

UNIT 12

À l'hôtel

You would narrow your search to just one or two-star hotels, prix toutes taxes comprises, de (très) bonnes tables

Vocabulary builder

un appartement, un gîte rural, une chambre d'hôte

Practice

1 a 2, **b** 14, **c** 12, **d** 6, **e** 4, **f** 8, **g** 16, **h** 11, **i** 1, **j** 10, **k** 9, **l** 3, **m** 5, **n** 7, **o** 13, **p** 5, **2 a** the hotel might be full **b** two nights **c** tout de suite

Conversation

3 a breakfast **b** yes **c** from 7.30 to 10 o'clock

4 a faux **b** faux **c** vrai **d** vrai **e** faux **5** Bonsoir, vous avez une chambre, s'il vous plaît? / Non, une chambre double à deux lits et avec salle de bains. / C'est pour quatre nuits. / C'est combien? / C'est quoi, une promotion? / Est-ce que le petit déjeuner est compris? / À quelle heure servez-vous le petit déjeuner? / On peut prendre un repas dans l'hôtel? / Haussmann, c'est qui? **6 a** Le radiateur ne marche pas **b** Il n'y a pas de savon **c** Il n'y a pas d'eau chaude **d** La lampe ne marche pas **e** Il n'y a pas de serviettes **f** La douche ne marche pas **g** La télévision ne marche pas **h** Il n'y a pas de couvertures **8 a** Yes, John's reservation has been accepted, but it won't be guaranteed until he pays the safety deposit **b** Combien de personnes peuvent dormir dans le gîte? **c** Est-ce qu'il faut amener du linge de maison / des draps, des serviettes? **d** Est-ce que vous acceptez les chiens? **e** Qu'est-ce qu'il faut faire pour garantir la réservation? **9 a** gîtes ruraux et chambres d'hôtes **b** until 1 September **c** kitchen utensils and household linen

Test yourself

1 a étoiles **b** réserver **c** marche **d** caution **e** ascenseur **2 a** Avez-vous des chambres de libre? **b** Est-ce que l'hôtel accepte les animaux? **c** C'est combien, la chambre? **d** Est-ce que l'internet est compris dans le prix de la chambre? **e** Vous servez le petit déjeuner dans la chambre?

UNIT 13

Manger au restaurant

1 a 2, **b** 3, **c** 4, **d** 1 **2 a** can easily **b** simple **c** meat and a side of vegetables **d** a limited range of dishes **e** the daily special **f** pancakes

Vocabulary builder

Je voudrais mon bifteck bien cuit. / Vous avez du jus d'ananas?

Conversation

3a a croque monsieur is a grilled ham and cheese sandwich. **b** une omelette aux champignons **c** je crois que je vais prendre **d** une pression et un café crème **4** 6 **a** 3 **b** 1 **c** 5 **d** 2 **e** 4 **f 5** Je voudrais un croque-monsieur / Vous avez des omelettes? / Qu'est-ce que c'est 'Parmentier'? / Je vais prendre l'omelette Parmentier / Qu'est-ce que vous avez comme jus de fruit? / Je voudrais un jus d'ananas et l'addition, s'il vous plaît. **7 a** He orders from the 33€ menu. **b** onion soup **c** yes it is, it comes with a side of beans, carrots and green salad **d** medium **8 a** Vous avez une table pour une personne? **b** Je crois que je préfère ... **c** Vous le voulez comment? **d** Vous pouvez me conseiller pour le vin? **e** Vous avez choisi un dessert? **f** Amenez l'addition après le dessert. **9** Pour commencer je vais prendre un filet de hareng. / Alors je vais prendre un avocat à la vinaigrette. / Qu'est-ce que c'est le cassoulet? / Je n'aime pas les haricots. Je préfère la grillade du jour avec frites. / À point. Je voudrais aussi une bouteille de Sauvignon. / Qu'est-ce que vous avez comme desserts? **g** Je vais prendre une glace à la vanille. / Qu'est-ce que vous avez comme autres parfums? / Je vais prendre une glace à la fraise.

Test yourself

1 a Qu'est-ce que vous avez comme snacks? **b** Nous préférons la bière en bouteille, **c** Je voudrais un jus de pomme, s'il vous plaît. **d** Avez-vous choisi une entrée? **e** J'aime ma viande bien cuite. **f** Vous pouvez m'apporter l'addition, s'il vous plaît? **g** Il n'y a/il ne reste plus de jambon. **h** Qu'est-ce que vous avez comme parfums de glace? **2 a** glace **b** omelette **c** boulangerie **d** cassoulet

UNIT 14

Getting round Paris

Buy a **carnet** or a **carte Paris visite**

Vocabulary builder

a métro **b** gare routière **c** aller-retour **d** horaire **e** guichet **f** voyage/trajet **g** billet

1 a Où est-ce qu'il faut prendre le bus? **b** Je voudrais voyager dans la matinée. **c** Est-ce qu'il faut changer de ligne de métro? **d** Quelle ligne de RER va à l'aéroport Charles de Gaulle?

Practice

1 a Où est-ce qu'il faut prendre le bus? **b** Je voudrais voyager dans la matinée. **c** Est-ce qu'il faut changer de ligne de métro? **d** Quelle ligne de RER va à l'aéroport Charles de Gaulle? **2 a** vous pouvez parlez plus lentement, vous pouvez répéter? **b** vrai **c** faux **d** faux **3 a** direction **b** prenez **c** changer **d** mener **e** manquerez **4 a** He's not from the town. **b** It's 500m away. **c** straight on **5 a** 2, **b** 1, **c** 3, **6 a** acheter **b** carnets **c** magasins **d** ligne **e** tickets **7** She's encouraged to buy a carnet, which is cheaper. **8** She needs to get off at the first stop after crossing the Seine. **9 a** C'est quelle ligne pour aller à la Gare d'Austerlitz? **b** C'est direct? **c** C'est loin à pied? **d** Le prochain bus part à quelle heure? **e** Où est-ce que je peux acheter un ticket? **f** Je voudrais acheter un (ticket) aller-retour pour les Invalides. **g** Je vais prendre un carnet. **h** Il faut combien de temps pour arriver à la gare? **10 a** to Marseilles **b** the 9.20 train **c** by the window

Language discovery

Je suis dans le train

11 Je voudrais un (billet) aller-retour pour Paris le 8 octobre l'après midi. / Il (le train) met combien de temps? / Je ne veux pas arriver à Paris après 19 heures / Le train de 15.29 me convient. C'est combien le billet en deuxième classe? / C'est un peu cher. Il y a (quelque chose de) moins cher? / Le train arrive à Paris à quelle heure? / C'est trop long./Ça met trop de temps. Je vais prendre le train de quinze heures vingt.

Test yourself

1 a correspondance **b** côté **c** réduction **d** matinée **e** descendez **2 a** Je voudrais un carnet. **b** Je voudrais un aller-retour pour Grenoble. **c** C'est quelle direction pour (aller à) la Gare d'Austerlitz? **d** Le prochain bus part à quelle heure? **e** Où est-ce que je peux acheter un billet? **f** Il faut combien de temps pour le trajet/voyage? **g** Il faut que je réserve/je dois réserver une place?

UNIT 15

Vocabulary builder

tarif réduit, hors saison, le dimanche nous faisons une promenade/balade à vélo/ viens faire une promenade/balade avec nous.

1 a see the monuments, walk along the Loire river, take the children to the swimming pool, visit the Science museum or the Floral Park **b** Je voudrais un plan de la ville. **c** Qu'est-ce qu'il y a à voir? **d** Qu'est-ce qu'il y a à faire pour les enfants? **e** Il y a une piscine couverte? **f** Pour aller au Parc Floral, il y a un bus? **2 a** 4, **b** 5, **c** 6, **d** 8, **e** 3, **f** 1, **g** 7, **h** 2, **3 a** les moins de 18 ans **b** most, admission, free, seniors, teachers **4 a** carte **b** librement **c** monuments **d** offices **e** forfait **5 a** B **b** A, C and D: on the 1st Sunday of each month **c** A: every evening except Tuesdays until 9 p.m. + late-night openings with some exhibitions; C: late-night opening on Wednesdays and Fridays; D: late-night opening on Thursdays; **d** B because of its dynamic approach in teaching sciences and techniques: interactive games, spectacles, etc. **6 a** 7.15 a.m. **b** one hour **c** have lunch, visit the Hospices, the wine museum and the wine cellar **d** 184€ **7** Nous voulons faire l'excursion de la route des vins de Bourgogne. / Nous voulons deux places pour le 22 juillet. / Le car part d'ici? / Vous pouvez répéter, s'il vous plaît? / Merci. À quelle heure part le car? / On peut acheter du vin dans la cave? **8 a** dimanche **b** 9.15 **c** 7 heures environ **d** le matin: visite des appartements du château et des jardins, déjeuner dans le restaurant du Château, l'après-midi: visite du Grand Trianon et du petit village construit pour la Reine Marie-Antoinette **e** Le prix de l'entrée est compris dans le prix de l'excursion. **f** Michel offre l'excursion à Agnes parce que c'est son anniversaire.

Test yourself

1 a Je voudrais un plan de la ville et des renseignements sur la cathédrale. **b** Le parc est facile à trouver? **c** Est-ce que le musée ferme entre midi et deux heures? **d** Il faut être à l'arrêt de bus à quelle heure? **2** climatisé, bateau, journée, inclus, thème, gratuitement, soirée **3 a** Qu'est-ce qu'il y a faire ici? **b** Le musée est ouvert les jours fériés? **c** C'est gratuit pour les moins de dix-huit ans? **d** Tu viens faire une balade à pied? **e** La visite prend combien de temps?

UNIT 16

Looking for entertainment

a pastime/form of entertainment, a ski instructor, a beach game, enjoy the good weather

Vocabulary builder

cours means *lesson*, **court** is *a tennis court*

2 a F in the evenings **b** F they like to dance and eat well **c** F it is a restaurant with music, open all night **d** V **e** V **f** V **3 a** E **b** D **c** C **d** B **e** A **4 a** Monday **b** his wedding anniversary **c** dinner by candlelight **d** Spanish **e** 2 a.m. **f** a dozen red roses **5 a** 5, **b** 6, **c** 8, **d** 1, **e** 2, **f** 7, **g** 3, **h** 4 **6** Where can you play tennis? Where can you book a court? How much is it per hour? Does the club rent rackets? What's the address of the club? **7 a** Où est-ce qu'on peut jouer au tennis? **b** Où est-ce qu'on réserve le court? **c** C'est combien l'heure? **d** On peut louer une raquette? **e** Vous pouvez/Est-ce que vous pouvez/Pouvez-vous me donner l'adresse du club, s'il vous plaît? **8** She gets a student discount. **9 a** Je voudrais des places pour dimanche prochain. **b** Ça finit à quelle heure le concert? **c** C'est combien la place? **d** C'est tarif réduit. **e** Ma sœur doit payer? **10 a** 1 yes **2** no; **b** 1 yes **2** no; **c** 1 no **2** yes; **d** 1 yes **2** no; **e** 1 play table tennis **2** board games

Test yourself

1 a Qu'est-ce qu'on peut faire ici? **b** C'est complet le concert de ce soir? **c** C'est combien l'heure (pour un court de tennis)? **d** On peut louer l'équipement de golf au club? **e** Qu'est-ce qu'il y a comme jeux de société? **2 a** pédestre **b** abonnement **c** à vélo **d** dansante **e** particulier **f** société **g** location **h** réduit

UNIT 17

La banque et l'euro

en province / windows, gates and bridges / openness and co-operation

The Euro 'made in France'

1 a No, different coins are minted in each country of the euro zone. **b** One side shows national symbols, **c** un centime **2** b, d and e

Vocabulary builder

Vous pouvez changer dix euros, svp? / Il me faut deux pièces de deux euros.

5 a vous n'avez pas de carte bancaire? **b** Il me faut cinq pièces de 1€ **c** elle (la machine) n'accepte que... **d** vous pouvez changer...? **e** Je n'en ai pas (de carte). **f** Je ne sais pas. **g** Ça vous va? **h** vous avez de la chance **i** je vais regarder **6 a** No, she's not carrying enough change. **b** She gives him a coin. **c** She has children of her own, she knows what it's like.

7 a bureaux **b** devises **c** voyage **d** change **e** bancaire **8** Je voudrais changer des dollars. / Des dollars américains. / Des billets. / 200 dollars. C'est quoi le taux de change aujourd'hui? / Il y a une commission à payer? **9 a** 5€40 **b** 7€22 **c** 19€75 **d** 22€ **e** 89€56 **f** 172€ **g** 315€40 **h** 632€15 **i** 918€30 **j** 72 centimes **10 a** drinks from the mini-bar appear on the bill **b** after breakfast **c** 14 **d** a mini-bar charge **e** yes

Test yourself

1 a 10, **b** 5, **c** 6, **d** 2, **e** 9, **f** 1, **g** 4, **h** 3, **i** 8, **j** 7 **2 a** 3, **b** 4, **c** 2, **d** 5, **e** 1

Vocabulary builder

J'ai mal

2 a He's got a sore throat and a headache. **b** No, he's not running a fever. **c** throat lozenges, aspirin, toothpaste, and sun cream **3 a** 2, 4 **b** No **c** 3, 4 **d** 3 two every four hours and 4 one when needed **4** Ma fille a mal aux dents. / Oui, un peu. / Depuis hier. / Merci. Vous avez quelque chose pour les piqûres d'insectes? / Je vais la prendre; c'est combien?

Le service médical

the doctor, la feuille de soins

5 a She's calling about her daughter **b** a violent headache **c** a **consultation** takes place at the surgery, a **visite** is a house call / the doctor is busy (lit. is taken) all day **6** b, c, e, f **7** 3**a** 8**b** 1**c** 6**d** 2**e** 4**f** 9**g** 5**h** 10**i** 7**j** **8 a** clés **b** stylo, lunettes **c** portefeuille, cartes **d** identité **e** téléphone **f** voiture, faire **9** Volvo, S70, AB08 PLM **10 a** on m'a volé ma voiture **b** C'est quoi votre voiture? **c** Quel est le numéro d'immatriculation? **d** faire une déclaration par écrit **e** remplir cet imprimé **f** vous en avez besoin pour vos assurances.

Test yourself

1 a 5, **b** 3, **c** 1, **d** 2, **e** 4 **2 a** je voudrais prendre rendez-vous avec le docteur **b** J'ai mal au ventre. **c** Je souffre/J'ai mal depuis trois jours. **d** Je ne peux pas manger. **e** Je peux venir demain à 10 heures. **3 a** perdu **b** laissé **c** a volé **d** sont cassées **e** oublié

French–English vocabulary

à *to, in*
abord *see* **d'abord**
abricot *(m) apricot*
acceuil *(m) welcome*
accord *see* **d'accord**
achat *(m) shopping;* **faire des achats** *to do some shopping*
acheter *to buy*
addition *(f) bill, sum*
adorer *to adore, to love*
adresse *(f) address*
affaires *(f pl) business;* **homme d'affaires** *businessman;* **femme d'affaires** *businesswoman*
âge *(m) age*
agence de voyages *(f) travel agency*
aider *to help*
aimer *to like, to love*
aire *(f)* **de pique-nique** *picnic area;* **de jeu** *playground*
alcool *(m) spirit*
alimentation *(f) grocer's shop*
aller *to go*
aller *(m)* **simple** *single ticket*
aller-retour *(m) return ticket*
allô *hello (on the phone)*
alors *well, then*
ambiance *(f) atmosphere*
amener *to bring something or somebody*
ami *(m),* **amie** *(f) friend*
amende *(f) fine*
an *(m) year;*
anchois *(m) anchovy*
ancien(ne) *ancient, former*

anglais(e) *English (often used for British)*
Angleterre *(f) England*
année *(f) year*
animal *(m)* **animaux** *(pl) animal(s)*
août *August*
apéritif (apéro) *(m) before dinner drinks*
apparaître *to appear*
appareil photo *(m) camera*
appartement *(m) flat*
arrondissement *(m) municipal or administrative district*
s'appeler *lit. to be called;* **je m'appelle** *my name is*
apprécier *to appreciate*
apprendre *to learn*
après *after*
après-demain *(m) the day after tomorrow*
après-midi *(m) afternoon*
argent *(m) money*
arrêt *(m) stop*
arrivée *(f) arrival*
arriver *to arrive*
arrondissement *(m) district in large towns*
ascenseur *(m) lift*
aspirine *(f)* **effervescente** *soluble aspirin*
assez *enough, fairly*
assiette *(f) plate*
attendre *to wait for;* **en attendant** *in the meantime*
aujourd'hui *today*
au revoir *goodbye*

aussi *also, too, as well*
autobus *(m) bus;* en autobus *by bus*
autocar *(m) coach;* en autocar *by coach*
automne *(m) autumn;* en automne *in autumn*
autoroute *(f) motorway*
autre *other;* autre chose *something else*
avec *with*
avion *(m) aeroplane*
avoir *to have;* avoir l'air *to seem*
avril *April*

baguette *(f) 'French stick' (bread)*
se baigner *to go for a swim*
balade *(f)* à pied *a pleasure walk* en bateau *a boat ride*
balle *(f) ball*
banlieue *(f) suburb*
banque *(f) bank*
bar *(m) bar*
bas(se) *low*
bas *(m) bottom, lower part*
basket *(m) basketball*
bâtiment *(m) building*
battre *to beat*
beau (belle) *handsome, beautiful*
beaucoup (de) *much, a lot*
belle *see* beau
besoin *(m) need;* avoir besoin *to need*
beurre *(m) butter*
bien *well;* bien sûr *of course*
bientôt *soon;* à bientôt *see you soon*
bière *(f) beer*
bijouterie *(f) jeweller's*
billet *(m) ticket, (bank) note*
blanc (blanche) *white*
bleu(e) *blue;* bleu marine *navy blue;* bleu pâle *pale blue*
blond(e) *blond*
bœuf *(m) beef, ox*
boire *to drink*

boisson *(f) drink*
boîte *(f) box, can, tin*
boîte *(f)* aux lettres *letter box*
boîte *(f)* (de nuit) *disco, nightclub*
bol *(m) bowl*
bon(ne) *good;* bon marché *cheap*
bonjour *good day, hello*
bonsoir *good evening*
bord *(m) side, edge;* au bord de la mer *at the seaside*
botte *(f) boot*
boucherie *(f) butcher's*
bouchon *(m) cork, bottleneck*
boulangerie *(f) baker's*
boulevard *(m) boulevard*
bout *(m) end;* au bout de *at the end of*
bouteille *(f) bottle*
brasserie *(f) pub-restaurant*
briller *to shine*
britannique *British*
brosse à dent *(f) toothbrush*
brouillard *(m) fog*
bruit *(m) noise*
brun(e) *brown (hair, complexion)*
bureau *(m)* de location *box office*
bureau *(m)* de renseignements *information office*
bureau *(m)* des réservations *booking office*
bureau *(m)* de tabac *tobacconist-cum-newsagent's*
bus *(m) see* autobus

cabine *(f)* d'essayage *fitting room*
cabine téléphonique *(f) telephone box*
cabinet de toilette *(m) small room containing wash basin and bidet*
cadeau *(m) present*
café *(m) coffee, café;* café au lait *white coffee;* café crème *coffee served with cream;* café du coin *corner café*
caisse *(f) cash desk, cashier's ticket office*

ça *that, it;* **ça va?** *how are things?;* **ça va** *things are OK*

campagne *(f) country;* **à la campagne** *in (to) the country*

camping *(m) camping, campsite*

car *(m) see* **autocar**

carnet *(m) book (of tickets), ten metro tickets*

carrefour *(m) crossroads*

carotte *(f) carrot*

carte *(f) map, card, menu;* **carte bancaire** *banker's card;* **carte d'abonnement** *season ticket;* **carte de crédit** *credit card;* **carte d'identité** *identity card;* **carte postale** *postcard*

cassé(e) *broken*

caution *(f) security country*

ce, cet, cette *this, that (adjective)*

ceci *see* **ce**

célèbre *famous*

célibataire *(m and f) single, bachelor*

cent *a hundred*

centime *(m) centime*

centre *(m) centre;* **au centre de** *in the centre of;* **centre ville** *town centre,* **centre commercial** *shopping centre*

certain(e) *certain*

certainement *certainly*

ces *these, those*

c'est *it is, this is*

c'est ça *that's it*

cet, cette *see* **ce**

ceux *those (who)*

chambre *(f) bedroom*

champignon *(m) mushroom*

chance *(f) luck;* **avoir de la chance** *to be lucky*

changer *to change*

changeur *(m)* **de monnaie** *coin changing machine*

chaque *each, every*

charcuterie *(f) shop selling*

cooked meats

chaud(e) *hot;* **avoir chaud** *to be hot*

chauffer *to heat up*

chauffeur *(m) driver*

chaussure *(f) shoe*

chemise *(f) shirt*

chèque *(m)* **de voyage** *see* **traveller**

cher (chère) *expensive, dear*

chercher *to look for;* **aller chercher** *to fetch*

cheveux *(m pl) hair*

chez *at the home of;* **chez moi** *at my house, at home*

chiffre *(m) number*

chocolat *(m) eating or drinking chocolate*

choisir *to choose*

choix *(m) choice*

chose *(f) thing*

cinq *five*

cinquante *50*

circulation *(f) traffic*

citron *(m) lemon*

classe *(f) class*

classique *classical*

clé *(f) key*

coffre-fort *(m) safety box, safe*

coin *(m) corner*

combien (de)? *how much? how many?*

commander *to order*

comme *as, like, in the way of*

commencer *to start, to begin*

comment *how, how to, what*

commissariat (de police) *(m) police station*

complet(ète) *full*

composer *to dial (a telephone number)*

composter *to date-stamp (a ticket)*

comprendre *to understand*

comprimé *(m) tablet*

compris *understood, included*

comptable *(m) accountant*

concert (m) concert
concombre (m) cucumber
connaître to know (a person or a place)
connu(e) known
conseiller to advise
consigne (f) left luggage; consigne automatique luggage lockers
consultation (f) a doctor's/dentist's appointment
content(e) pleased
continuer to continue
convenir to suit; ça me convient it suits me
copain/copine (boy, girl) friend
correspondance (f) connection
costume (m) suit for men
côté (m) side; à coté de next to; de l'autre côté on the other side
se coucher to go to bed
couchette (f) couchette
couleur (f) colour
coup (m) de fil telephone call
courriel (mail) (f) email
cours (m) particulier private lesson
cours (m) du change exchange rate
courses (f pl) shopping, errands
court(e) short
court (m) de tennis tennis court
coûter to cost
couverture (f) blanket, cover
cravate (f) tie
crème (f) cream; crème solaire (f) sun cream
crêperie (f) pancake house
croire to believe
croissant (m) croissant
croque-monsieur (m) toasted cheese sandwich with ham
en cuir in leather
cuisine (f) kitchen, cooking
cuit(e) cooked; bien cuit(e) well done

d'abord firstly

d'accord OK, agreed
dans in, into
danser to dance
date (f) date
de of, from
décembre December
décider to decide
déclaration (f) statement
décrocher l'appareil to lift the receiver
déjeuner to lunch, lunch; petit déjeuner (m) breakfast
demain tomorrow
démarrer to start
demi(e) half; demi-kilo (m) half a kilogram; demi-heure (f) half an hour
dent (f) tooth
dentifrice (m) toothpaste
dépannage: le service de dépannage breakdown service
dépendre de to depend on
dépenser to spend (money)
depuis since; je suis marié depuis dix ans I've been married for ten years
déranger to disturb, to inconvenience; en dérangement out of order
dernier(ière) last
derrière behind
descendre to go down
désirer to wish for, to want
désolé(e) sorry
desservir to serve
détester to hate
deux two
deuxième second
devant in front of
devise (f) currency; devise étrangère foreign currency
devoir must, should, ought
différent(e) different
dimanche Sunday
diminuer to decrease
dîner (m) dinner, to have dinner; dîner

aux chandelles *candle-lit dinner*
dire *to say*
direct(e) *direct*
directement *directly*
direction *(f) direction, management*
directeur (directrice) *manager*
disque *(m) record*
distributeur automatique *(m) cash point, ATM*
se divertir *to be entertained*
divertissement *(m) entertainment*
dix *ten*
dix-huit *18*
dix-neuf *19*
dix-sept *17*
doit, ça doit *see* **devoir**
donc *therefore*
donner *to give*
dormir *to sleep*
douche *(f) shower*
douze *12*
droguerie *(f) ironmonger's, hardware store*
droit(e) *straight;* **tout droit** *straight on*
avoir droit *to be entitled*
à droite *right (hand)*

eau *(f) water*
eau *(f)* **minérale** *mineral water;* **gazeuse** *sparkling water*
école *(f) school*
écouter *to listen*
écrire *to write*
par écrit *in writing*
église *(f) church*
élève *(m and f) pupil*
émetteur(trice) *issuing*
emmener *to take (someone somewhere)*
emplacement *(m) pitch*
en *in, on, of it, of them*
encore *again*
enfant *(m and f) child*
ennuyeux(se) *boring, tedious*

enseignant(e) *teacher*
ensemble *together*
ensemble *(m) outfit, suit (woman)*
ensuite *then*
entre *between*
entrée *(f) way in, admission charge; starter course*
environ *about*
environs *(m pl) surroundings*
envoyer *to send*
épeler *to spell*
équitation *(f) horse riding*
erreur *(f) mistake*
espérer *to hope*
essayer *to try*
essence *(f) petrol*
essuie-glace *(m) windscreen wiper*
est *(m) east*
et *and*
étage *(m) floor*
été *(m) summer;* **en été** *in summer*
étoile *(f) star*
étranger (étrangère) *foreigner;* **à l' étranger** *abroad*
être *to be*
eux *them (people)*
éviter *to avoid*
excursion *(f) excursion, trip;* **faire une excursion** *to go on an excursion*
excuser *to excuse*
expliquer *to explain*
en face (de) *facing*

facile *easy*
faim *(f) hunger;* **avoir faim** *to be hungry*
faire *to do, to make*
famille *(f) family*
il faudra *it will be necessary*
il faut *it is necessary, one has to*
faux (fausse) *false*
favori (te) *favourite*
femme *(f) wife, woman*

fenêtre (f) window
fermé(e) closed
fermer to close
fête (f) feast-day, celebration
feux (m pl) (de circulation/rouge)
    traffic lights
février February
fièvre (f) fever, temperature
figurer to appear
fille (f) daughter, girl
fils (m) son
finalement finally
finir to finish
flèche (f) arrow
flûte (f) flute
fleur (f) flower
fois (f) time; une fois once
fond (m) back, far end; au fond du
    couloir at the far end of the corridor
fondre to melt
forêt (f) forest
forfait transport (m) travel pass
forme (f) shape; en pleine forme fully
    fit
formidable great
formulaire (m) form
foulard (m) scarf
fourchette (f) fork
fraise (f) strawberry
français(e) French
France (f) France
frère (m) brother
frein (m) brake
frite (f) chip; (adjective) fried
froid(e) cold; avoir froid to be cold
fromage (m) cheese
fruit (m) fruit

garçon (m) boy, waiter
garder to keep
gare (f) station; gare routière bus,
    coach station; gare SNCF railway
    station

garer to park
garni(e) served with vegetables, salads,
    etc.
à gauche left
généralement generally
gentil(le) kind, nice
géographie (f) geography
gérant (e) manager
gîte rural (m) self-catering cottage
glace (f) ice cream
glisser to slide
gonflage (m) des pneus pumping up
    the tyres
gorge (f) throat
gourmet (m) gourmet
grand(e) big, tall
Grande-Bretagne (f) Great Britain
gratuit(e) free
grillade (f) grilled meat
grippe (f) flu
gros (grosse) fat, large
guichet (m) ticket office
gymnastique (f) gymnastics

(s')habiller to dress
habiter to live
haricot (m) bean; haricot vert green
    bean
heure (f) hour; quelle heure est-il?
    what time is it?
histoire (f) tale, history
hiver (m) winter; en hiver in winter
homme (m) man; homme d'affaires
    businessman
homologué classified
hôpital (m) hospital
horaire (m) timetable
hors outside; hors-d'œuvre starter; hors
    de service out of service
hôtel (m) hotel; hôtel de ville town hall,
    hôtel de luxe luxury hotel
huile (f) oil
huit eight

ici *here*
île *(f) island;* Île de France *Paris area*
indicatif *(m) dialling code*
indiquer *to indicate*
informatique *(f) IT*
ingénieur *(m) engineer*
inscription *(f) enrolment*
intéressant(e) *interesting*
introduire *to insert*
inviter *to invite*

jamais *never*
jambon *(m) ham*
janvier *January*
jardin *(m) garden*
jardinage *(m) gardening*
jaune *yellow*
jean *(m) or* jeans *(m pl) jeans*
jeu *(m) game;* jeu de société *board, parlour game*
jeudi *Thursday*
jeune *young*
joli(e) *pretty*
jouer *to play*
jour *(m) day;* jour de l'an *New Year's Day;* jour férié *bank holiday;* de jour *by day*
journal *(m) newspaper*
journée *(f) day, day-time*
joyeux(se) *joyful, merry*
juillet *July*
juin *June*
jupe *(f) skirt*
jus *(m)* de fruit *fruit juice*
jusqu'à *until, as far as*

kilo(gramme) *(m) kilogram*

la *the, her, it*
là(-bas) *(over) there*
lait *(m) milk*
laisser *to leave;* laissé *left*
large *wide, big*

(se) laver *to wash*
le *the, him, it*
léger (légère) *light*
légume *(m) vegetable*
lentement *slowly*
lequel, laquelle *who, which;* sur laquelle *on which*
lettre *(f) letter*
leur(s) *their, to them*
se lever *to get up*
liaison *(f) link, relationship*
librairie *(f) bookshop*
libre *free (but for free of charge use* gratuit*);* libre service *(m) small supermarket*
ligne *(f) number (bus), line (metro)*
limonade *(f) lemonade*
linge de maison *(m) house linen*
lire *to read*
lit *(m) bed;* à deux lits *twin-bedded;* le grand lit *double bed*
litre *(m) litre*
livre *(m) book; (f) pound*
location *(f) hire, rental*
logement *(m) lodgings*
loin *far*
loisir *(m) hobby, pastime*
long (ue) *long*
louer *to let, to hire, to book*
lourd(e) *heavy*
lui *to him, to her, he, as for him*
lundi *Monday*
lunettes *(f pl) glasses,* lunettes de soleil *sunglasses*

Madame *Madam, Mrs*
Mademoiselle *Miss*
magasin *(m) shop;* grand magasin *department store;* magasin de chaussures *shoe shop*
mai *May*
maillot *(m)* de bain *swimming costume, swimsuit*

maintenant *now*

mais *but*

maison *(f) house;* **à la maison** *at home;* **maison de campagne** *(f) country house*

mal *badly;* **avoir mal** *to have a pain;* **mal** *(m)* **de dos** *backache*

malheureusement *unfortunately*

manger *to eat*

manifestation culturelle *(f) cultural event*

manquer *to be lacking, missing*

marchand(e) *seller, vendor*

marché *(m) market;* **bon marché** *cheap*

marcher *to walk, to work (for a machine)*

mardi *Tuesday*

mari *(m) husband*

marié(e) *married*

marron *brown*

mars *March*

matin *(m) morning*

matinée *morning time*

mauvais(e) *bad*

médecin *(m) doctor, physician*

médicament *(m) medicine*

meilleur(e) *better ;* **meilleur marché** *cheaper*

mélange *(m) mixture*

mélanger *to mix*

même *same, even*

menu *(m) set meal*

mer *(f) sea;* **au bord de la mer** *at the seaside, by the sea*

merci *thank you*

mercredi *Wednesday*

mère *(f) mother*

Messieurs-dames *ladies and gentlemen*

mesurer *to measure*

métro *(m) underground*

mettre *to put*

meublé *furnished*

mi-temps *part-time*

midi *midday, lunchtime*

mieux *better*

milieu *(m) middle, milieu*

mille *a thousand*

mince *thin*

minuit *midnight*

modèle *model*

moi *me, I*

moins *less*

mois *(m) month*

moitié *(f) half*

mon, ma, mes *my*

monde *(m) world;* **tout le monde** *everybody*

monnaie *(f) small change*

Monsieur *Sir, Mr*

montagne *(f) mountain;* **à la montagne** *in, to the mountains*

monter *to go up*

montre *(f) watch*

montrer *to show*

monument *(m) monument*

morceau *(m) piece*

moteur *(m) engine*

motif *(m) pattern, design*

moyen(ne) *medium, average*

musée *(m) museum*

musique *(f) music;* **musique classique** *classical music*

natation *(f) swimming*

navette *(f) shuttle*

il neige *it's snowing*

neuf *nine*

neuf (neuve) *new*

niveau *(m) level*

nocturne *late-night opening*

Noël *(m) Christmas*

noir(e) *black*

nom *(m) name*

nonbreux(ses) *many, large, plentiful*

non *no*
nord *(m) north*
normal(e) *normal*
note *(f) bill (hotel, telephone)*
notre, nos *our*
nouveau(elle) *new;* à nouveau *again*
novembre *November*
nuit *(f) night;* de nuit *by night*
numéro *(m) number;* numéro
    d'immatriculation *number plate*

occupé(e) *busy*
s'occuper *to deal with, to attend to*
octobre *October*
œil *(m) eye*
œuf *(m) egg*
œuvre *(f) work of art*
office du/de tourisme *(m) tourist office*
omelette *(f) omelette*
on one *(used also for we and I)*
oignon *(m) onion*
onze *11*
(en) or *(made of) gold*
ordonnance *(f) prescription*
ou *or;* ou ... ou *either ... or*
où *where*
ouest *(m) west*
oui *yes*
ouvert(e) *open*
ouvre-boîte *(m) can/tin opener*
ouvrir *to open*

pain *(m) bread*
paire de chaussures *(f) pair of shoes*
panne *(f) breakdown;* en panne *broken
    down*
panneau *(m) sign*
pantalon *(m) trousers*
paquet *(m) packet*
paquet-cadeau *(m) gift-package*
parcmètre *(m) parking meter*
parce que *because*
pardon *pardon, sorry, excuse me*

parfum *(m) perfume, flavour (ice cream)*
parking *(m) car park*
parler *to speak*
en particulier *particularly*
partir *to go, to leave*
à partir de *from, as*
pas *not;* pas du tout *not at all*
passant(e) *passer-by*
pastille *(f) lozenge*
pêche *(f) peach*
pâté *(m) pâté;* pâté de campagne
    country pâté
pâtisserie *(f) a cake shop, pastry, cake*
patrimoine *(m) heritage, patrimony*
payer *to pay*
pays *(m) country, area*
à péage *toll payable*
pêche *(f) peach*
peigne *(m) comb*
pendant *during*
penser *to think*
perdre *to lose;* perdu(e) *lost*
père *(m) father*
personne *(f) person;* personne agée *(f)
    pensioner, senior;* personne (+ ne)
    nobody
perte *(f) loss*
peser *to weigh*
pétanque *(f) pétanque (kind of bowls)*
petit(e) *small;* petit déjeuner
    (m) breakfast
(un) peu *(a) little, few*
pharmacie *(f) chemist's*
pharmacien(ne) *(m, f) chemist*
pièce *(f) room, coin;* pièce d'identité
    personal ID
pied *(m) foot;* à pied *on foot*
pique-nique *(m) picnic*
piscine *(f)* (couverte) *(indoor)
    swimming pool*
place *(f) square, space, seat*
plaisir *(m) pleasure;* faire plaisir *to
    please;* avec plaisir *with pleasure*

plan *(m)* **(de la ville)** *(town) map*
planche *(f)* **à voile** *windsurfing board*
plat *(m)* *dish, course;* **plat du jour** *daily special ;* **plat principal** *maincourse*
plein(e) *full;* **le plein, s'il vous plaît** *(at the garage) fill it up, please*
il pleut *it is raining*
sans plomb *(m)* *lead-free petrol*
(la) plupart *most*
plus *more, plus;* **plus ... que** *more than;* **en plus** *in addition, extra;* **ne ... plus** *no longer, no more*
pneu *(m)* *tyre*
poêle *(f)* *frying pan*
poids *(m)* *weight*
à point *medium done (meat)*
point de repère *(m)* *landmark*
point-presse *(m)* *newsagent's*
pointure *(f)* *shoe size*
pois, petits pois *(m pl)* *peas*
poisson *(m)* *fish*
poivre *(m)* *pepper;* **poivrer** *to pepper*
poivron *(m)* *bell pepper*
pomme *(f)* *apple;* **pomme de terre** *potato;* **pommes frites** *(f pl) chips*
pompiste *(m)* *pump attendant*
ponctuel(le) *punctual*
pont *(m)* *bridge*
portail *(m)* *gateway*
portefeuille *(m)* *wallet*
porte-monnaie *(m)* *change purse*
porter *to carry, to wear*
poste *(f)* *post, post office*
poulet *(m)* *chicken*
pour *for, in order to*
pourboire *(m)* *tip*
pouvoir *can, be able to;* **vous pouvez** *you can*
pratique *practical, convenient*
pratiquer *to practise, to do, to play*
préférer *to prefer*
premier(ière) *first*

prendre *to take;* **pris(e)** *taken, busy*
présenter *to introduce*
près (de) *near;* **près d'ici** *nearby*
pressing *(m)* *dry-cleaner's*
pression *(f)* *pressure (tyre); draught (beer)*
presque *nearly*
printemps *(m)* *spring;* **au printemps** *in spring*
prier *to beg, to pray*
privé(e) *private*
prix *(m)* *price*
prochain(e) *next*
proche *near*
professeur(e) *(m, f)* *teacher*
profession *(f)* *profession*
profiter *to enjoy, to take advantage of*
projet *(m)* *plan ;* **projet d'avenir** *future plan*
promenade *(f)* **(à pied)** *walk*
province *(f)* *region;* **en province** *outside Paris*
se promener (à pied) *to go for a walk*
publicité *(f)* *advertisement, advertising*
puis *then*
pull-over *(m)* *pullover*

quai *(m)* *platform*
quand? *when?*
quarante *40*
quatorze *14*
quatre *four*
quatre-vingt-dix *90*
quatre-vingts *80*
que *that, than*
(ne) ... que *only*
quel(le)? *which?, what?*
quelque(s) *some (a few);* **quelque chose** *something*
quelquefois *sometimes*
quelqu'un *someone*
qu'est-ce que *what*
qui *who, which*

quinzaine *(f) 15 or so*
quinze *15*
quitter *to leave*
quoi? *what?*

raide *straight (hair)*
ramener *to bring back*
randonnée *(f) hike*
rapide *rapid*
raquette *(f) racket*
réceptionniste *(m/f) receptonist*
réduction *(f) discount*
regarder *to watch*
régon parisienne *(f) Greater Paris*
régler *to settle (bill)*
regretter *to be sorry*
remplir *to fill in*
rendez-vous *(m) appointment*
rendre *to give back;* **rendre la monnaie**
    to give change
rendre visite *to pay a visit*
renseignement *(m) (piece of)*
    information
se renseigner *to enquire*
rentrer *to go back, to go home*
réparer *to repair*
repas *(m) meal*
répéter *to repeat*
répondre *to answer*
se reposer *to rest*
RER *(m) fast extension of the*
    underground in the suburbs
réseau *(m) network*
restaurant *(m) restaurant*
restauration rapide *(f) fast-food*
réserver *to reserve, to book*
rester *to stay*
retard *(m) delay;* **en retard** *late*
retirer (de l'argent) *to withdraw*
    money
retourner *to go back, to return*
rien *nothing;* **de rien** *don't*
    mention it

robe *(f) dress*
rocade *(f) ring road, bypass*
rond(e) *round*
rouge *red*
route *(f) road*
RSVP *RSVP*
rue *(f) street*

sac *(m)* **à main** *handbag*
saignant(e) *bleeding, rare (meat)*
saison *(f) season;* **hors saison**
    out of season; **en pleine saison**
    in high season
saler *to salt*
salle *(f) hall, auditorium, room;*
    salle de bains *bathroom;*
    salle à manger *dining room*
sandwich *(m) sandwich*
sans *without*
saucisse *(f) sausage*
saucisson *(m) kind of salami*
savoir *to know (a fact or how to do*
    something e.g. **je sais faire la**
    cuisine *I know how to cook)*
savon *(m) soap*
scène *(f) scene*
séance *(f) session*
sèche-cheveux *(m) hair dryer*
second(e) *(adj) second*
secrétaire *(m and f) secretary*
seize *16*
sel *(m) salt*
selon *according to*
semaine *(f) week*
sens *(m) direction, way, meaning*
sept *seven*
septembre *September*
servir *to serve*
serviette *(f) towel, napkin;* **serviette de**
    toilette *hand towel*
serveur (serveuse) *(m) waiter, server*
shampooing *(m) shampoo*
s'il vous plaît *please*

situé(e) *situated*

six *six*

ski *(m) ski;* **ski de fond** *cross-country skiing;* **ski de piste** *downhill skiing*

SNCF *(f) French railways*

sœur *(f) sister*

soie *(f) silk;* **en soie** *made of silk*

soif *(f) thirst;* **avoir soif** *to be thirsty*

soir *(m) evening*

soirée *(f) evening, evening entertainment*

soixante *60*

soixante-dix *70*

en solde *in the sale*

soleil *(m) sun*

son, sa, ses *his, her, its*

sortie *(f) exit*

sortir *to go out;* **sortir en boîte** *to go clubbing*

souci *(m) worry, concern*

souffrir *to suffer*

source *(f) spring (of water)*

souvenir *(m) souvenir, memory*

souvent *often*

spécial(e) *special*

spectacle *(m) show*

sport *(m) sport*

station *(f)* **de métro** *underground station,* **station thermale** *spa*

stationnement *(m)* **(interdit)** *(no) parking*

stationner *to park*

station-service *(f) petrol station*

stylo *(m) pen*

sucre *(m) sugar;* **sucreries** *(f pl) sweet things*

sud *(m) south*

suivre *to follow*

supermarché *(m) supermarket*

sur *on*

surtout *mainly, especially*

svp (s'il vous plaît) *please*

sympathique *friendly, pleasant*

syndicat d'initiative *(m) tourist office*

table *(f) table ;* **une bonne table** *a good restaurant*

taille *(f) size, waist*

tard *(adv) late*

tarif *(m) price list, rate;* **tarif réduit** *reduced rate*

tarte *(f) pie*

taux de change *(m) exchange rate*

taxi *(m) taxi*

télécarte *(f) phone card*

téléphone *(m) telephone*

téléphoner (à) *to phone*

télévision *(f) television;* **télé**

temps *(m) time, weather;* **à plein temps** *full-time*

tête *(f) head*

T.G.V. *(m) high speed train*

thé *(m) tea*

thon *(m) tuna*

ticket *(m) ticket*

timbre *(m) stamp*

tir à l'arc *(m) archery*

tire-bouchon *(m) corkscrew*

toi *you (familiar)*

toilette *(f),* **faire sa toilette** *to wash and dress;* **les toilettes** *lavatory*

ton, ta, tes *your*

tonalité *(f) dialling tone*

tôt *(adv) early*

toujours *always*

touriste *(m and f) tourist*

tourner *to turn*

tout(e), tous, toutes *all;* **tout de suite** *immediately;* **tout droit** *straight ahead;* **tout le monde** *everybody;* **tous les deux** *both of them;* **tous les jours** *every day*

train *(m) train;* **en train** *by train*

traiteur *(m) caterer*

trajet *(m) journey*

tranche *(f) slice*